THE
HITTING
EDGE

THE HITTING EDGE

Tom Robson

Human Kinetics

Library of Congress Cataloging-in-Publication Data

Robson, Tom, 1946-
  The hitting edge / Tom Robson.
      p.   cm.
Includes index.
    ISBN 0-7360-3336-X (Soft Cover)
  1. Batting (Baseball)   I. Title.
  GV869 .R63   2003
  796.357'26--dc21   2002153990

ISBN: 0-7360-3336-X

Developmental Editor: Cynthia McEntire; **Assistant Editors:** Carla Zych, John Wentworth; **Copyeditors:** Barbara Walsh, Barbara Field; **Proofreader:** Coree Clark; **Indexer:** Gerry Lynn Messner; **Graphic Designer:** Robert Reuther; **Graphic Artist:** Francine Hamerski; **Photo Managers:** Carl D. Johnson, Dan Wendt; **Cover Designer:** Keith Blomberg; **Photographer (cover):** © Associated Press; **Photographer (interior):** Tom Roberts except where otherwise noted; **Art Manager:** Dan Wendt; **Illustrators:** Dick Flood, Brian McElwain; **Printer:** Phoenix Color Corporation

On the cover: John Olerud of the Seattle Mariners hits a two-run homer off Oakland A's pitcher Tim Hudson in the fourth inning, September 30, 2001.

Human Kinetics books are available at special discounts for bulk purchase. Special editions or book excerpts can also be created to specification. For details, contact the Special Sales Manager at Human Kinetics.

Printed in the United States   10 9 8 7 6 5 4 3 2 1

Human Kinetics
Web site: www.HumanKinetics.com

United States: Human Kinetics
P.O. Box 5076
Champaign, IL 61825-5076
800-747-4457
e-mail: humank@hkusa.com

Canada: Human Kinetics
475 Devonshire Road Unit 100
Windsor, ON N8Y 2L5
800-465-7301 (in Canada only)
e-mail: orders@hkcanada.com

Europe: Human Kinetics
107 Bradford Road
Stanningley
Leeds LS28 6AT, United Kingdom
+44 (0) 113 255 5665
e-mail: hk@hkeurope.com

Australia: Human Kinetics
57A Price Avenue
Lower Mitcham, South Australia 5062
08 8277 1555
e-mail: liahka@senet.com.au

New Zealand: Human Kinetics
P.O. Box 105-231, Auckland Central
09-523-3462
e-mail: hkp@ihug.co.nz

To David and Adam for being great sons and class individuals who have always believed in me

To my mom, my angel in Heaven

To my dad, the greatest man on Earth

CONTENTS

FOREWORD

While I was growing up, baseball was one of my favorite sports. It came easy to me, and I enjoyed a fair amount of success throughout high school and college. I didn't have a very complicated swing—rock the hands back as the pitcher delivered the ball and try to drive it back up the middle or to the opposite field.

In 1989 I signed with the Toronto Blue Jays and started my professional career. In my first few years in the major leagues, I worked hard to establish myself as an everyday player. I kept the same approach to hitting that I had growing up, which resulted in some decent years. In 1993, my breakout year, everything went my way. I was hitting the ball to all fields, hitting for average and power, and driving in runs. I won the batting title and hit .400 into the month of August. I thought I knew how to hit.

Well, the next three years were a real struggle. Hitting the ball to all fields, which at one time was so natural for me, now felt foreign. I got into some bad mechanics by trying to pull the ball too much and really got out of sync. I worked hard with the hitting coaches, but I was never able to turn things around. I was on my way out of baseball unless I got my swing back.

In December 1996, I was traded to the New York Mets. I had gone from hitting .363 in 1993 to .275 in 1996. I knew that I needed to get back to hitting the ball to all fields but did not know where to start. Then I met Tom Robson. Tom was the hitting instructor for the Mets and helped me turn my career around. He noticed some flaws in my swing and helped me to use my lower half more effectively. Tom had specific things for me to work on. It wasn't the same old clichés like "stay back" or "use your hands." He had something that really worked. He knew the mechanics of the swing, how the swing worked, and how to get the most out of it. He knew a lot of the bad habits people get into, how to make the corrections, and most importantly he kept it simple. Because of Tom's instruction, I got my swing back and saw results. In 1998 I hit .354, finishing second in the batting race.

Tom Robson is the best hitting coach I've had in my professional baseball career. *The Hitting Edge* is your personal guide to the same instruction Tom provided me in the most productive years of my playing career. I encourage you to learn and apply what he teaches in the pages that follow. Work on each area diligently in practice and you'll soon see results. You might not reach the big leagues but you can reach your hitting potential. Let Tom show you the way.

John Olerud

ACKNOWLEDGMENTS

Special thanks to Bobby Valentine, my manager for 14 years in the Major Leagues, including Japan. No one knows more about the game of baseball. What little I've learned has bounced off him onto me.

I want to thank Ralph Dickenson, minor league hitting coordinator with the Brewers, Expos, and currently the Texas Rangers. He talks hitting and constantly challenges me with thoughts and ideas on how to improve all types of hitters, from Little League to Major League. I thank him for his insight and knowledge on the art of hitting.

Thanks to Tim Foli, third base coach for the Cincinnati Reds, for his love and knowledge of baseball and for being a true friend.

Thanks to Bob Keyes, director of the Utah Baseball Academy and owner of BioKinetics, for letting me have input with the data and analyses of all types of players for research and information to help me understand what really happens with the swing.

Special thanks to Dr. Tom House, for always being there to help and for introducing me to the clinic scene.

A very special thanks to John Olerud, a great player, a great hitter, and an even greater family man. Thank you, John, for the trust and the friendship. You are the definition of a class act.

Thanks to Randy Niemann, my fellow coach with the New York Mets, for letting me see the lighter side of this game of baseball and keeping me organized and sane during a long Major League season.

My favorite comedian, Steven Wright, once said, "I wrote a children's book, but not on purpose." So, last, a great big thank you to my editor at Human Kinetics, Cynthia McEntire, for making sure I did not write a children's book.

INTRODUCTION

Ted Williams, probably the greatest hitter who ever lived, said that the most important thing for a hitter to do is get a good pitch to hit. I think Ted was right. In *The Hitting Edge,* we will cover the preparation that hitters need before that good pitch is thrown to the plate.

Proper preparation prevents poor performance. An unprepared hitter will have a hard time being consistently successful at the plate, even if he does get the right pitch to hit. A prepared hitter who has proper mechanics, the right attitude, and good pitch recognition has a better chance of putting the ball in play.

Today's players are bigger, stronger, and faster than they've ever been before. Major league records that everyone thought were untouchable are being broken. Even so, at every level of baseball, coaches still debate and argue about the best way to teach the art of hitting. If you put 25 coaches together in a room and ask them to discuss hitting, you're certain to witness some heated arguments. It's a subject people have strong opinions about, and that's the way it's been for a long time.

Baseball is a traditional sport. We hold onto a lot of old teachings too long, which sometimes does a disservice to our players. Even with all the scientific information we have at our disposal today, baseball coaches find little common ground when they talk about hitting. Some of the information out there is very good. Most baseball coaches have great intentions and work hard to improve their players, but good intentions must be backed up by good information.

Coaches need to find the best information possible so their players can make the jump to the next level—high school varsity, junior college, major college, or even the major leagues. Coaches have to supply players with good enough information so that players can achieve the highest level that their talent and drive can take them.

In *The Hitting Edge*, I want to make it simpler to teach, learn, and execute the art of hitting a moving baseball. I want to give you the information that can help you achieve as high a level as possible.

I've been lucky in this game. I've played at many levels—possibly every level of baseball ever invented. I played in Little League, went on to Pony League, played American Legion ball, played in high school, won a national championship at the junior college level, and played major college ball. I signed professionally and played A ball, double-A, triple-A, and a little bit in the major leagues. I know what it takes to get to each of these levels. I know what it takes for a hitter to hit at all of these levels.

I've played all over the world—in Japan, Mexico, Canada, and Puerto Rico. I've played with and coached players from all over the world. I saw Ichiro Suzuki while I was coaching in Japan in 1995-1996. When he made it to the United States in 2001, he took the major leagues by storm. More Japanese players will come to the United States in the next few years because they want to learn more about baseball and play the game at the highest level in the world.

I've coached some of the greatest players in the world. Three or four will probably be in baseball's Hall of Fame one day. It's pretty remarkable to work with players of that caliber. Mike Piazza, Ivan Rodriguez, and Rafael Palmeiro are three players I believe have a good chance of being elected to the Hall of Fame. I was fortunate enough to work with those hitters at various points in their careers while I was coaching with the Texas Rangers and the New York Mets.

I've also had good teachers. Every player has someone who helped him over the hump. It might have been a Little League coach, a high school coach, or a coach at any level. I learned more about baseball from Bobby Valentine than anyone else I've ever been around. He was the manager of the Texas Rangers from 1985 to 1992 and invited me to join him in the big leagues in 1986. Bobby has also taught me most of what I know about the art of hitting, He has a keen eye for detail and can spot a hitter's flaw even before he sees it on slow-motion videotape. He pushed me to become more aware of the actual happenings of a hitter rather than just the absolute mechanics. With good information, a coach can learn the mechanics and drills a hitter needs to improve, but a real coach can know and understand exactly what he's looking at when he sees the hitter in a practice or competitive situation. That's what makes a coach successful—knowing what you're looking at in a hitter and then instantly relaying a simple message to the hitter to keep him in line or bring him back to the right path. Bobby taught me how important it is to handle hitters differently and how crucial it is to provide all hitters with the best possible information available at the correct time to breed success.

Everyone has to have someone in life to get them over the hump or push them to another level. A hitter may run into that person in high school or college and go on to have a great career; a youngster may run into that person in Little League and go on to have a fun time just playing baseball in high school. In both cases, there is great accomplishment and great success.

Bobby taught me at the professional level, which proves it is never too late to learn about the different phases of baseball and improve skills. I'll always have respect for Bobby.

I know what good hitters do. I know what happens during the swing. I know how the body works to create energy and bat speed. I'm still learning today. Every day we're collecting more data on the best players in the world.

Every hitter has an individual hitting style. I'm not trying to create clones; every hitter is unique in his own way. Let me introduce a theme that I'll keep coming back to throughout this book: It's not how you do it, but if you do it. Style is great, but it's time to figure out what's really important to becoming a good hitter.

Hitting a baseball is the most difficult and ballistic skill in sports. Teaching hitters has become so complicated that coaches try to make clones and robots out of young hitters. If there were one right way to hit, everyone in the major leagues would hit the same way, but they don't. The difficult responsibility of the hitting coach is to provide the facts about hitting while at the same time maintaining the unique styles of young players.

In *The Hitting Edge,* the science of hitting is integrated with the art of hitting. It isn't just how a hitter does it—it's when and if he does it. With modern technology, a hitter's swing can be scientifically analyzed, providing an objective, science-based perspective into the hitter's strengths and weaknesses. This knowledge can be combined with the hitter's ambition, hard work, and desire to create a dangerous hitter who approaches every at bat with purpose and determination.

By integrating sport science research and objective baseball information, coaches can concentrate on the real problems of hitting, not just treat the symptoms of bad habits. All coaches should want to know exactly what happens during the swing and how the body works. A coach with this kind of knowledge can give better instruction to his hitters, giving them a real chance to become better.

To hit a baseball successfully, an athlete must master four separate but linked skills: mental, perceptual, reactional, and mechanical. Each skill is of equal importance; if a player is deficient in any of the four, he will struggle at the plate.

Mentally a hitter must have a plan for each at bat. He must be confident, in control of his emotions, and aware of the game situation. This combination of confidence, control, and awareness makes up the hitter's attitude. A hitter with attitude and a game plan is mentally prepared to step into the batter's box.

When the pitcher begins his delivery, hitting becomes a perceptual skill. At this point, all of the hitter's energy goes into seeing the ball as well as possible. Once he sees the ball, he has only a split second to react to it. His reaction time is affected by genetics, functional strength, and conditioning. A hitter who has physically trained his body to swing the bat with mechanical efficiency is more likely to be successful.

Let's say a hitter who wants to improve decides to take a hundred swings a day. If he takes a hundred quality swings a day, after a while he's going to be a little better than when he started. If he takes a hundred bad swings a day, not knowing that he is etching bad habits, he's going to be worse than when he started. If a hitter who knows what's important in the swing takes a hundred quality swings a day, he'll get much better. I know what good hitters do, and now you will, too.

CHAPTER 1

Attitude

ulio Franco was one of the best hitters I've ever coached. As a Texas Ranger, Franco won the batting title in 1989 with a .341 batting average. He had what I call a hitter's attitude. He was cocky and arrogant at the plate. He just knew he was going to get a hit. Even when he had a bad at-bat—striking out or swinging at a pitch in the dirt—he would come back to the dugout with a tiny smile on his face, sit down, and say, "You know what, I really stunk that time. But let me tell you something—that pitcher's in real trouble next time." Franco always carried that attitude. He hit the ball hard more often than anyone I've ever coached.

Many hitters I've coached have had that hitter's attitude, including Ruben Sierra, Rafael Palmeiro, Brian Downing, and many more. Most good hitters carry an attitude with them to the plate. Some hitters, like Julio Franco, just show it more openly than others.

Every hitter must be ready to compete and perform. A hitter may have to deal with poor conditions, a particularly good pitcher, his own slumps and doubts, fatigue, and the like. It is essential to know how to deal with any situation that may arise. Good preparation is essential to good performance.

An experienced hitter who has prepared physically and mentally is ready to perform to his top potential. Physical preparation requires a commitment to success with good mechanics, solid conditioning, and proper practice. Mental preparation consists of clearing the mind of all negative thoughts and being able to focus on the ball every at bat and every pitch.

Physical conditioning is simply preparing the body to perform the necessary task. It is neuromuscular programming for the skill of hitting a baseball during competition. A hitter must be able to maintain balance while swinging a bat at high speed. He must train his body to work in sequence. He must develop the rotational skills necessary to fire a bat through the hitting zone at the exact same time the baseball is in that zone. Taking practice seriously and working hard on all phases of the game require discipline, a very important element in the physical and mental development of good hitters.

This discipline in physical preparation helps foster the integration of mind and body in mental preparation. Proper mental preparation creates "game intelligence," and a smart hitter often can outperform a more talented hitter. Preparing mentally means having a swing plan for each pitch in every at bat, clearing the mind of all negative thoughts,

Rafael Palmeiro carries a hitter's attitude to the plate for every at bat.

and focusing on the ball no matter what the game situation is. A hitter who is physically and mentally prepared to hit is not afraid of failure and can be very aggressive with every swing he takes.

THE REAL DEFINITION OF ATTITUDE

A good hitter has a presence at the plate—what I call the *hitter's attitude*. The hitter's body language shows that he has confidence in himself. Let's examine what attitude is before we discuss what it isn't.

Attitude is that slightly arrogant swagger a hitter displays as he approaches the plate. A hitter who isn't afraid to look a pitcher in the eye, or who keeps his head up even with two strikes or after a really bad swing, shows that he's not intimidated by anything that a pitcher might have for him. A good hitter never shows the pitcher that he's frustrated or worried about the situation. A hitter with the right attitude will look the same when he comes to the plate 0 for 5 as he does when he is 4 for 5.

Although a hitter needs to be arrogant and cocky at the plate, that doesn't mean he should talk trash. He should be able to look the pitcher straight in the eye and say to himself, "Come on, let's go. Come get me." Attitude is an inner confidence that shows in the way the hitter physically carries himself.

A good hitter shows the attitude even when he doesn't feel it. There isn't a hitter alive who feels good all the time. Every hitter will have many times when he doesn't feel right in the box—doesn't feel in control. Think about your own experiences. Maybe at times you feel tired or a little intimidated by a wild, hard-throwing pitcher. Maybe you hear your parents screaming for you to get a hit. Suddenly your thoughts turn to things beyond the current at bat, and your concentration is shattered.

That's when a good hitter has to fake it. Don't let the pitcher see you with your head down. If he sees you like that, he'll become more confident; he'll be the one in control. Even when you feel afraid or lack confidence due to a slump, or have other things on your mind that interfere with your thought processes, you must always remember to display the hitter's attitude. It must be there when your girlfriend is in the stands or a scout is watching or a recruiter is following you. It must be there every time you step up to the plate.

Confidence

Which comes first, confidence or hits? Do you gain confidence by getting hits, or do you get hits because you have confidence? The best answer I can give is that it depends. Each hitter is unique. Are you self-motivated, able to create confidence internally without any external demonstration of success? Or are you goal oriented, someone who needs to perform well to gain confidence? Play this game long enough and you'll find out which type you are. Don't worry, though. Either type of player can be successful. Even in the major leagues, there are both types of players.

Remember, you don't have to talk trash to show confidence. If you do talk trash, I have just one piece of advice: You'd better be really, really good. As you advance through different levels of play, you're going to have to be able to walk the walk and back up your words with action.

Preparation builds confidence, and a confident hitter will more consistently put a good swing on a good pitch.

A hitter's attitude is simply his presence at the plate. Even if he is not the sort to show cockiness on the outside (and many players are not), he still must feel it inside. If he does not have that feeling, he has to fake it. Do not let the pitcher see doubt, fear, or confusion because he will know you are in trouble and will feel in complete control of the at bat.

Many good hitters also display a calming attitude. For a couple of years, John Olerud was the calming force on the Mets. No matter how tense the situation or how important the game was, John always went to the plate with a look of "Everything's going to be okay," and he usually delivered.

Attitude is not an easy thing to measure because it comes from within the hitter himself. Coaches must help hitters believe in themselves and stay strong and positive through the good times and the bad times.

Although I love my hitters to death and have lived and died with their performances, I have to admit that the most amazing baseball player—indeed, the most amazing athlete—I've ever been around was a pitcher. Nolan Ryan had heart and desire and was the ultimate competitor. He had an unbelievable work ethic. Talk about taking information, working at it, and having the desire to be successful—Nolan Ryan had it all. Role models are hard to find these days, but you don't have to look any further than Nolan Ryan to find someone to admire.

John Olerud has been a calming force in the dugout and an offensive force on the field for the Blue Jays, Mets, and Mariners.

I was there for two of his no-hitters and was in the dugout for his 300th win and his 5,000th strikeout. What people didn't see was the way he prepared for each game and the work he put in to reach his goals. Not everyone is blessed with his arm, strength base, or genetic makeup. He was a very special man. But the way he handled himself with the younger players, the way he took over a game, and the methods he used to prepare himself for games were just the way things should be done. Ryan had the attitude, the desire, the heart, and the competitiveness to be great. He took charge of games and game situations—exactly what hitters should do. Hitters must learn to believe in themselves and have confidence in their abilities as hitters, just as Nolan Ryan did as a pitcher.

One of Ryan's rituals before the first pitch of the game was to get the ball and walk toward home plate. He would kick around at some spots in the grass about 20 feet from home plate, where a hitter could possibly bunt for a hit. He would then rub the ball in both hands while staring the first hitter of the game, who was waiting in the on-deck circle, dead in the eyes. It got to the point where leadoff hitters would just drop their heads and look the other way. Ryan had the advantage right then because he was in effect telling the hitter not to bunt and implying, "See where I am? Don't bunt it here because I don't like that." That was how he intimidated hitters, and he did it well.

Not everyone can be like Nolan Ryan, but his career demonstrates how the mental part of the game can lead to success. A hitter must have that hitter's attitude and body language that says, "I can hit whatever you throw." I want all hitters to have that kind of attitude.

Everything you do will be tempered by your attitude. Take the best information in the world, use it, and be as good as your potential will allow. As a hitter, you may hear people say you can't hit feet first, hands last. They'll tell you that the hands are the most important part of hitting. You may hear little about rotation and sequence. It's up to you to decide what's important and what's not. You'll have the ammunition to make the right decisions. Always listen to your coach, as he'll make suggestions that can help you succeed. Just be smart and filter out any information that you know won't help.

Even young kids can demonstrate the right attitude. Kids sometimes show such determination and energy to accomplish simple tasks, and it's fun to watch how their minds work. Youngsters can develop an

Ivan Rodriguez exemplifies confidence at the plate.

attitude early, as long as we adults do not hold them back and try to keep them silent.

The song "The Greatest" by Kenny Rogers illustrates the right attitude to have. The song is about a little boy who takes a bat and ball and plays a game in his mind, in which he sees himself as the greatest player of them all. He throws the ball up and swings with everything he's got, but he misses as the ball falls to the ground. He tells himself that he is the greatest and tries again. He throws the ball up and swings with all his might, but the ball falls to the ground for strike two. Not to be deterred, he gathers himself together, grits his teeth, and, hearing the cheers in his mind, throws the ball up one more time. He swings the bat and takes his best shot, but the ball falls to the ground for strike three. Just then his mother calls him in for supper. As he picks his stuff up to go home, he says to himself, "I'm still the greatest, but even I didn't know I could *pitch* like that!" Now that's an attitude that finds good even when there seems to be nothing but bad!

Young hitters need to be taught a hitter's attitude, especially the difference between trash talking or bragging and an inner strength that keeps them on the right track and leads them down the road to success. Hitters such as Julio Franco, Gary Sheffield, and Ivan Rodriguez outwardly show confidence and cockiness, but they respect their opponents. They just feel like they're better than any pitcher and go about trying to prove it!

There is nothing wrong with being good. How you handle that success says a lot about your character, and your attitude says a lot about you!

BUSTING OUT OF A SLUMP

A slump is a prolonged stretch during which a hit can't be found or even bought. Going 0 for 10 does not signify a slump, although to some major league hitters and most young players, going 0 for 4 can become a major slump in their own minds. Almost all slumps are mental, but coaches and players try to fix a slump by changing physical elements of the swing, such as the stance or approach. It is essential to understand the nature of slumps and deal with them by using the mind.

I have seen many major league players hit two or three line drives for outs and then try to figure out what's wrong with their swings. Little league players often get discouraged if they go 0 for 3 or get two strikeouts, thinking this is a major slump. They end up trying 10 different things to get back on track, when in fact they never left the track in the first place. Trying to change the mechanics of a hitter to fix an 0 for 5 begins a vicious cycle that never goes away and will be there for as long as a player chooses to play.

Deal with the mind first. That means having a clear head and seeing the ball correctly. Always think *this pitch, this moment*. Believe in yourself and show confidence even when you doubt. Never, and I mean never, be afraid to swing and miss. Always take your best swing, and confront one pitch at a time and deal with it. This pitch, this moment is all a hitter can deal with at any given time. A hitter's mechanics should be changed only if something is interfering with one of the absolutes of hitting: dynamic balance, sequential rotation, axis of rotation, and bat lag.

We will cover the absolutes in more detail in later chapters, but briefly, dynamic balance means controlling the center of gravity from start to finish; sequential rotation means using the body in the correct order, feet first, hands last; axis of rotation means keeping a strong posture; and bat lag means pulling the bat through the zone as the last link in the swing.

When slumping, older players may reach rock bottom, resigning themselves to just going out and playing because they think they can't get any worse. Then the hits return because they finally have learned to relax and see the ball as it should be seen. There is no need to ever sink that low, because a poor performance can be changed in a short amount of time with some common sense, self-confidence, and good work habits.

Remember, a so-called slump results from mental mistakes more often than physical ones. Often the hitter loses focus and has no idea what he's trying to do at the plate. Keep in mind, though, that going 0 for 5 is not a slump; that's going to happen many, many times during the course of a season. How the hitter deals with an 0 for 5, or even an 0 for 15, will determine how long he is stuck in his slump.

Focusing on this pitch, this moment can get a hitter out of a slump very quickly. What has happened in the past is over and done with. What is about to happen is the only thing that matters. The sooner we learn this, the better we'll be as coaches and as hitters.

The benchmark today, as it has been for years, is that a .300 hitter is a good hitter. That means even a good hitter fails 7 out of 10 trips to the plate. So even a good hitter is going to fail 70 percent of the time. That doesn't sound so bad, but put it in perspective. A major league hitter who has 600 at bats will walk back to the dugout 420 times without a hit. Wow! He makes more than 400 outs and still gets paid all that money! That just shows how difficult it is to hit a little white ball moving at top velocity.

So hitters have to deal with this failure. They cannot let failure affect the next at bat or even the next pitch. A hitter must be able to take a bad swing or have a bad at bat but still move on to the next pitch or at bat and be successful. He has to have an attitude.

A hitter can't let a poor performance carry over into the next opportunity. Pouting or feeling sorry for yourself when you're in a slump can become a habit, starting a vicious cycle that's very hard to break.

A younger player who strikes out or swings at a bad pitch may retreat to the end of the bench, shake his head, and think, "What am I doing wrong?" All kinds of negative thoughts run through his mind. Good hitters keep the hitter's attitude even when the at bat doesn't generate the desired result.

As soon as I can, I try to break hitters of the habit of feeling sorry for themselves. A good hitter must have a positive attitude. Many players have prevented themselves from advancing to a higher level of play because they couldn't handle failure. Good hitters learn to deal with it.

RETURNING FROM INJURY

Injuries are a part of sports and must be dealt with intelligently. Trying to work through an injury that needs time to heal can cause a lot of bad habits.

Coming back from a major injury can be tricky. The mistake most athletes make is coming back too soon and getting hurt again. A good rehab program is essential for complete recovery. All good programs include specific movements that pertain to the sport and actions of that sport, abdominal work to rebuild stability and balance, and rotational movements that allow a hitter to recover his swing more quickly.

While with the White Sox, Robin Ventura suffered a horrible ankle injury but was able to return to the game thanks to hard work and sound medical treatment.

© Anthony Neste

A hitter must maintain his strength base while allowing the injured part of his body to heal correctly.

After the injury heals and the hitter reaches normal strength, he must then get back to regaining his swing. More important, he has to redevelop his timing and recognition skills. Just as a hitter who takes off the winter months has to relearn to time a baseball and recognize all pitches, a player returning from injury must do the same.

Coming back from an injury is not difficult if a lot of work and a little common sense are incorporated on the road back to excellence. Robin Ventura, now with the New York Yankees, came back from a devastating ankle injury and continues to excel at the major league level three and four years later.

Returning to competition after a major injury is common in this day and age, with all the new treatments and rehab techniques. Be smart and ask the experts for advice. With dedication, hard work, and good medical treatment, the body usually will respond positively.

Lesser injuries are those nagging pains that come along with playing every day or over a prolonged time period. These injuries usually have to run their course, and you'll get through them okay. A good rule is that if you warm up and get loose and the pain lets up or disappears, you were just stiff from a previous activity. If the pain gets worse, stop and take care of whatever aches correctly. That means treatment, heat, whatever the doctor or trainer recommends, until you are ready to go again.

Be smart about injuries and take the time necessary to completely heal before going full speed in a game. Know the difference between being hurt and being stiff. If you're stiff and take the time to warm up, you'll find that the stiffness seems to go away. If that stiffness never leaves the area, even after a good stretching or throwing warm-up, then it's time to stop and have a physician look at the injured area.

It takes time to return from an injury and get back into the swing of things. A hitter must realize that he's not going to be exactly the way he was before the injury. Give yourself some time to get your timing, recognition skills, and swing back into shape without panicking if you happen to miss a few pitches you think you should have hit.

A lot goes into the development of a good hitter. It's not just how far the hitter can hit the baseball or if he shows up for a game to take his swings. It's preparing mind and body to do whatever's necessary to hit the ball hard and consistently. It's helping the team become better. Having a hitter's attitude and having fun while playing is what baseball is all about.

CHAPTER 2

Focus

A hitter learns in three ways: by listening, by seeing, and by feeling. The most efficient of these is feeling. A hitter must get to the point at which he can feel his legs working beneath him. He can feel dynamic balance and strong posture. A hitter must feel that he has good bat speed and quickness. A hitter feels many things during an at bat. With practice and experience, he'll learn to filter out wrong signals and allow his body to work correctly.

Experience teaches a hitter his strengths and weaknesses, and a good hitter will be able to use that to his advantage. A low-ball hitter, for example, will look for the ball down low in the strike zone and be ready to attack any type of pitch in that area.

Experience requires input. The more input a hitter is given, the better hitter he will be. Small things contribute to experience. For example, watching the pitcher warm up and pitch to other batters can help a hitter prepare before coming to the plate. Shadow swinging from the on-deck circle gives a hitter the chance to time the pitcher's game tempo, revealing the pitcher's rhythm and release point. This knowledge will allow the hitter to be more aggressive at the plate.

Experience also means knowing situations. For the pitcher, the game situation dictates pitch selection and location. For the hitter, the game situation may dictate the purpose of the swing—moving runners along, working the pitch count, executing a bunt or a hit-and-run.

"Sudden" Sam McDowell, a great pitcher with the Cleveland Indians and a good friend of mine, used to say, "This pitch, this moment." Many hitters have taken Sam's saying to heart. The only thing you deal with during an at bat is this pitch, this moment. That's all you have to focus on. Once a pitch crosses the plate, that pitch is gone forever, whether you swung at it in the dirt or whiffed at it over your head. Clear your head so you can see the ball as it should be seen.

If you're focusing on the game situation—bases loaded with two outs in the bottom of the ninth, for example—or if you're worried about driving in base runners, or if you're listening to somebody yelling at you from the stands, then you're not concentrating on the task at hand. You'll be way ahead of the game if you learn to focus at the plate for 10 to 15 seconds on this pitch, this moment, oblivious to everything else going on. The younger you are when you learn to do this, the more successful you're going to be. Deal with one pitch at a time.

This pitch, this moment doesn't mean you're looking for a specific pitch, a fastball or a breaking ball, for example. It simply means that you're focusing all your energy and attention on what is about to happen—nothing more. If the situation calls for a fastball, then you look for a fastball. This pitch, this moment is a state of mind. It isn't trying to figure out what pitch will be thrown.

This pitch, this moment is simply a phrase that helps hitters focus on the task at hand. A hitter can deal only with the next pitch, no matter what situations arise. If it's a bunt situation or the hit-and-run is in order, the hitter still deals with this pitch, this moment because to get the job done correctly, he has to have complete control of the situation. Different situations do not change the "this pitch, this moment" thought process.

It can be difficult for even an elite hitter to focus and concentrate at the plate because of the time factor involved with the swing. The hitter needs to concentrate and focus for only a short time period, usually only a few seconds per pitch. That sounds like it would be easy, but it's not. Even a split-second loss of focus or concentration can result in failure. A hitter has to stay diligent at the plate.

Compare this to focusing or concentrating in the field. If an infielder has a lapse in concentration and misjudges a ground ball, he still has a chance to knock it down and throw out the runner a good percentage of the time. An outfielder who does not see the ball off the bat right away and picks it up late can still run it down and make the catch much

The Bad-Ball Hitter

Vladimir Guerrero is the greatest bad-ball hitter I've ever seen. He can hit any breaking pitch on or over the plate, or even off the plate, with tremendous force. He's a rare athlete who has a poor concept of the strike zone but a phenomenal level of hand-eye coordination and great power and bat speed. His focus is solely on the ball itself; he really does not care much about the strike zone. "If I can reach it, I can hit it" seems to be his philosophy. Not many hitters can adopt this way of hitting. It takes a special athlete to be successful swinging at as many bad pitches as Guerrero does.

Good hitters such as Barry Bonds, Rafael Palmeiro, and John Olerud have developed great skills in recognizing pitches and know every aspect of the strike zone. Their focus and concentration allow them to see the ball as it should be seen (big and slow), while other hitters are trying to hit pitches that look like speedy golf balls (small and fast). At times, any hitter will lose the zone and chase pitches that are impossible to hit, but the key is that the great hitters do it less often than everyone else. That's what makes them great.

Barry Bonds has tremendous focus at the plate. He is able to see the pitch big and slow.

of the time. However, if a hitter misjudges the pitch in the 0.2 second he has to make a decision, he'll be out of luck for that pitch.

It is possible for a young hitter to learn to clear his mind and deal with those few seconds in time and space with great focus and purpose. A hitter who learns this skill has a much better chance of being consistently successful at the plate, regardless of the situation. Off-field distractions, such as a bad day at home or school, and on-field pressures, such as coming from behind or facing a particularly dominant pitcher, can be pushed aside, bringing the hitter back to this pitch, this moment.

Learning to concentrate on one pitch at a time (this pitch, this moment) and not dwell on what is going to happen or what just happened can cut down the margin of error for a hitter. Practicing with good visualization drills can really help the hitter focus on the task at hand. Once a hitter can learn to visualize different pitches and different locations while taking dry swings, he will be able to slow down the ball in his mind and see it as it should be seen. Seeing the ball shortly after it leaves the pitcher's hand will make the ball look slow and big. Picking up the ball late makes the ball look like a small golf ball, tiny and nearly unhittable, which can lead to swinging at pitches that are not in the strike zone.

Visualization is a useful tool. When a hitter can visualize all pitches in his mind, the real thing may seem easier and more familiar. He's seen every one of those pitches many times, so there are no surprises when he sees the real thing while standing in the batter's box.

One of my favorite drills is for the hitter to stand in against a pitcher when the pitcher is throwing his side work. This drill helps improve concentration and focus skills because everything is happening at close to true game speed. Picking up each pitch early and recognizing movement and speed comes from experience and a will to succeed. Remember, a good hitter wants to hit and will let nothing stop him from attacking the baseball without fear, doubt, or passivity.

A hitter who lacks focus and concentration usually will swing at pitches that aren't there. All hitters have swung at pitches over their heads or that bounce two feet in front of home plate. The reason for these idiotic swings is that the hitters did not see the pitches correctly. If they had, certainly they wouldn't have swung at the pitches in the dirt or over their heads. When the hitter's focus is out of whack, he can't even see what is happening in front of his own face.

Even elite hitters struggle with focus and concentration over the course of a season. John Olerud often tells me that he goes through periods during which he has no clue what he is doing at the plate. He doesn't see the ball well and feels like he is lost. This comes from a lack of focus and concentration, because his swing doesn't change from day to day (even if it feels like it does). Every hitter will go through this at some point during the season, but the good ones get back to a good concentration level sooner rather than later.

Track the pitch as far as possible into the hitting zone (figure 2.1). The head should not move very much, and the eyes must stay on the ball. A good hitter loses sight of the pitch 6 to 10 feet from home plate;

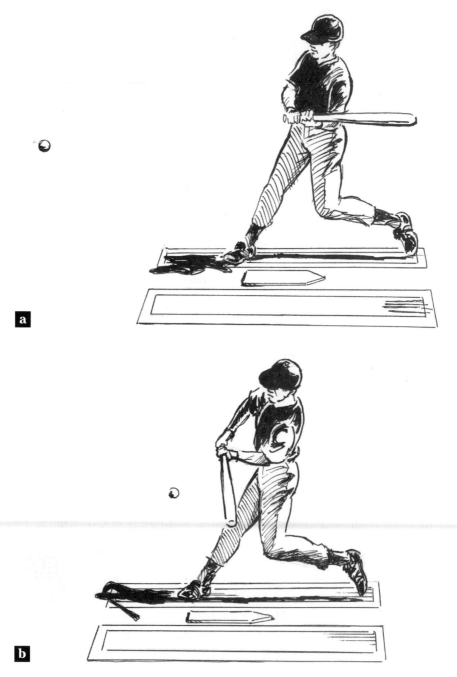

FIGURE 2.1   A successful hitter tracks the pitch into the hitting zone. He keeps his head still.

a bad hitter loses sight of it at 12 to 15 feet. If the hitter's head tries to follow the ball all the way into the catcher's glove as he tries to swing, he is defying one of the absolutes that allows the body to create force during motion—one body part cannot accelerate forward until another body part stops. The bat cannot attack forward to strike the ball if the head is moving back to track the pitch.

Keep your body posture strong. Keep your eyes level and still. Try to make the ball look big and slow (figure 2.2). Focus on the pitch as long as possible. Your body will rotate faster if you keep your head stable.

FIGURE 2.2   To a good hitter, the pitch looks big and slow.

Executing in a particular situation comes from practice and having the skills necessary to be successful. This pitch, this moment gives the hitter focus and concentration and is another tool available for success.

The problem many hitters have is that they overthink and try to figure out every possible scenario instead of letting their natural ability and preparation carry them to success. A pretty good hitter (say, around .300) who tries to figure out what went wrong with his swing every time he doesn't hit the ball hard or doesn't get a hit will be in misery most of the time. That's not much fun!

The goal is simply to block out unnecessary thoughts such as: "I have to get a hit or else!" "Don't screw up." "What happens if I strike out?" If a hitter can erase any unwanted thoughts and doubts from his head and just compete, and if he can narrow down any skill to this pitch, this moment, he will achieve a higher degree of success.

Learn to focus while you're young, and that talent of concentration will be there forever. Don't forget the principle of this pitch, this moment. Try to work it into your game plan. All you're going to deal with from this point on is this pitch, this moment.

Hitters must be able to take their concentration and intensity to the next level. Time, experience, and drills will help a hitter improve if he uses them. Use bullpen warm-up sessions to work on knowledge of the strike zone and pitch recognition skill (standing in versus a live pitcher). There is nothing like the real thing when it comes to seeing and recognizing different pitches.

Hitters who lack mental toughness and personal control usually are overreactive (hyper) to tough situations. A hitter needs to learn personal control and proper mental training to gain control of all situations. For example, how many times has a hitter wasted an at-bat because he was dwelling on a bad call made by the umpire? How many times has a hitter who just made an error in the field taken his disgust to the plate and given away an at-bat? The vicious cycle will go on forever until the hitter learns about himself and gains the confidence and arrogance—attitude—to control his own situation no matter what outside influences interfere.

Mental skills must be developed just as physical skills are developed. Good hitters do not leave this task to chance—they do something about it.

The mentally tough take responsibility for their thoughts and attempt to maintain consistency, which will be reflected by their actions and results. Consistency will come from learning to play the game one pitch at a time (this pitch, this moment); when one pitch is over, the hitter immediately prepares for the next pitch.

Visualize as many different scenarios as you can and make all of them successful executions in your mind. Trust your preparation once the game begins, and concentrate only on this pitch, this moment during competition.

CHAPTER 3

Timing

The most difficult thing to do in the entire world of sports is to hit a 90-mile-an-hour fastball. Robert Adair, a Yale physicist who studied the science of baseball for many years, said, "It's a superhuman feat that's clearly impossible." Hitting a baseball is very difficult, so hitters must prepare themselves to perform well.

Coach Bobby Valentine put it in perspective when he said, "A 90-mile-an-hour fastball travels from the pitcher's hand to the batter in a little more than four-tenths of a second. The first thing a hitter must do is decide if he's going to swing or duck." Sometimes the ball looks like it's coming dangerously fast. That's why many young hitters have to overcome fear to develop into consistent hitters.

Good timing means getting the body into a strong position so that when the stride foot lands, the ball is still far enough away. This allows the hitter to take his best swing at any pitch, at any velocity. A good hitter times the pitch, putting his body in the right place at the right time.

Timing and rhythm are crucial. You must be in a good balanced position to hit while the pitch is still far enough away for you to recognize it. Whatever kind of trigger you use—tap, kick, or stride—you have to start it early enough to give yourself as much time as possible to see the pitch. You must land on the balls of your feet at the correct time—when the ball is still about halfway to home plate—to give yourself as much time as possible to recognize the pitch.

When a hitter takes his stride and his front foot lands on the ground, the ball should be halfway between the mound and home plate (figure 3.1), or just a little past halfway and rushing at the hitter. The problem is, the hitter can't tell exactly where the halfway point is, but he does know that the ball isn't on top of him, and he does know the pitcher doesn't still have the ball in his hand. The ball is moving toward home plate. Now all the hitter has to do is recognize the pitch and begin a good, aggressive swing.

A hitter may not see the ball correctly if he's late or he feels everything is rushed. In contrast, to a hitter who has a 3-0 count and gets the take sign, the ball may look big and the pitch may seem extremely slow. He knows he's not swinging, so he relaxes. That's how the ball should look every single pitch. When young players learn that timing is just putting the body in the right place at the right time, the ball will look bigger and the pitch will seem slower.

You cannot increase bat speed or swing harder to catch up to extremely fast pitches. Your bat speed is not going to change from pitch to pitch. What you can change, however, is your timing. When facing a

FIGURE 3.1   The stride foot lands on the ground when the pitch is about halfway between the pitching mound and home plate.

hard thrower, don't try to swing harder. Start your rhythm and timing sooner, and the bat will have a chance to get to the ball on time. Begin a motion that will set up your swing. I don't mean you should commit early by bringing the bat head around or start the swing itself early. You must get your front foot down before the swing begins, and early motion allows you to stride to balance on time.

TRIGGERS

A hitter does only two things: he strides to balance, which is a linear movement, and he swings, which is a rotational movement. That's all a hitter does. Remember that.

As mentioned earlier, when the hitter's stride foot lands, the ball is about halfway to the plate. The batter is holding the bat over his shoulder, ready to fire, and he's in a good, strong launch position (figure 3.2).

FIGURE 3.2 A hitter in a good launch position holds the bat over his shoulder.

No Stride

Sometimes when a hitter is in the habit of lunging at the pitch, his coach will advise him to spread out or use no stride (figure 3.3). This quick fix will stop a hitter from lunging, but soon a few more weaknesses will appear.

The hitter will be more likely to get beat on anything inside. Since there is no initial movement, he has to hit from a dead stop. This goes against all the laws of physics that deal with motion. After getting beat a few times, the hitter will cheat with his upper body because the body knows it can't get there on time. This results in a poor sequence, which in turn leads to a slower bat.

FIGURE 3.3 The swing sequence with no stride.

Few hitters can get away with a no-stride approach. Paul Molitor and Moises Alou come to mind. Both of these hitters have an inner timing device that allows them to react in time with good pitches. No-stride hitters are definitely in the minority when it comes to being successful. Molitor and Alou can pull it off, but most hitters cannot. Most hitters need the stride to take them into rotation.

A coach can stop a hitter from lunging by teaching him that all good hitters hit against a firm front leg (see chapter 7). Once the stride foot lands, the body does not go any farther forward. Rotation begins at this time.

A Professional Negative Strider

Some hitters, such as Jeff Bagwell of the Astros, have an unusual setup and stance. Bagwell is very efficient at what he does. He has a negative stride, which means he steps backward and sits low with his stance. He gets his back foot off first and goes into a violent rotation with the correct sequence. That's why he usually has great years with above-average power.

© Anthony Neste

The Kick, Tap, and Traditional Stride

Good hitters have a trigger, something they do to get themselves into launch position. Employing this trigger, which is sometimes referred to as *loading up,* can be done many different ways. Some hitters tap the front foot, take a small step back, and then stride; others kick the front leg, get the leg up in rhythm, and put it down at the right time. Everyone has a different style.

In a major league game, you'll see hitters who tap, such as Chipper Jones and Sammy Sosa. You'll see kickers, such as Manny Ramirez and Todd Helton. You'll also see a lot of hitters who still take the traditional stride and approach.

Tip: A hitter cannot get aggressive until his stride foot lands on the ground.

Some of the best hitters I've seen with regard to timing are Rafael Palmeiro, Chipper Jones, and Juan Gonzalez. Two of these hitters—Palmeiro and Jones—use the tap as a trigger. Juan uses a leg kick. All have great flow with their approaches.

When I was with the Texas Rangers in the middle 1980s, I coached a few players who really got into using the kick as a setup or trigger. Players such as Ruben Sierra, Juan Gonzalez, Ivan "Pudge" Rodriguez, and Dean Palmer all used a kick to get ready to hit. Many people said, "The kickers are going to have problems with off-speed pitches. They're always going to be way out in front." But we proved just the opposite. Since the 1980s, the use of the kick as a timing device has increased tenfold among major league players.

These hitters use a kick as a trigger to get the body in a strong position to hit. A hitter who uses a kick has to start his stride earlier than one who uses a different style because the kick has more movement (figure 3.4). The hitter must be able to maintain his balance and keep his posture strong when he kicks up the leg. This means keeping his head over his center of gravity (the belly button) while going into and completing a strong, solid swing. Posture is key to successful hitting; it's a huge factor in maintaining proper balance and timing.

Using a kick to time the swing is not for everyone. Some hitters don't have enough stability to kick. If you can't hold your balance when you perform a kick or if you feel uncomfortable, don't use it. Remember, any style you choose must fall within your comfort zone and feel right to you.

Many young hitters try the kick simply because they've seen one of their favorite players use it. It's probably more difficult for very young players who are not physically developed yet. The kick requires more

FIGURE 3.4

Using the kick as a trigger. The front foot comes up.

The kick comes to its highest point before the leg moves forward.

FIGURE 3.4 *(continued)*

The head is stable as forward motion begins. The eyes are parallel to the ground.

The hitter strides to balance.

(continued)

FIGURE 3.4   *(continued)*

The front foot starts to open at foot landing.

Rotation begins and the back foot comes off.

FIGURE 3.4   *(continued)*

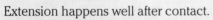

Extension happens well after contact.

The batter finishes high.

motion and timing during the approach, and younger hitters usually have insufficient coordination to achieve this.

High school and college players will have a better chance of succeeding with this method because they're stronger. If I were coaching an older player who lunged or jumped at the pitch, I would experiment with him using a kick, having him go to the back leg and kick to replace the lunge or jump. This would allow the hitter to stride to balance with better body control and begin rotation from a stronger position.

The height of the kick is unique to each individual player (figure 3.5). It can vary from about 4 to 6 inches in height to well above the belt buckle. The hitter must maintain dynamic balance from start to finish regardless of how high or low the kick is. Some studies show that the front leg displaces more energy at foot landing (i.e., goes into rotation

FIGURE 3.5   Different batters kick at different heights. If you choose to use the kick as a trigger, find the height that is comfortable for you.

with more force) when coming from a high kick as opposed to a regular straight stride or no stride at all.

If the hitter tends to drift forward prematurely, he can turn up his stride foot so that all or part of the bottom of the cleat faces the pitcher. This allows his upper torso to get completely over the back leg without drifting forward.

The body cannot start forward until the kick reaches its highest point (see figure 3.4, p. 32). Then the linear movement, the stride, can begin. Time the kick early enough to allow all the necessary movement to be completed on time.

The hitter should not stop at the height of the kick but rather should begin a slow transition into forward movement. In a practice setting, however, the hitter should be able to kick to his highest point and hold that position indefinitely. This is a good drill for practicing balance and body control.

The stride foot lands on the inside of the ball of the foot at close to a 45-degree angle (not closed or blocked off). Rotation begins just after the stride foot lands.

The kicker's posture should not change more than 2 to 2.5 inches away from a vertical axis of rotation, and his torso and head should stay in line with his center of gravity. The hitter should try to keep his eyes and head parallel to the ground (see figure 3.4, p. 33).

The hitter must learn to recognize the pitch while he is in motion. If the kick is done correctly, off-speed pitches should not be more of a problem for a kicker than for any other type of hitter.

The kick is a good trigger, but not everyone can do it. Rafael Palmeiro tried it, didn't like it, and went to the tap instead. He still uses the tap today as he hits his way to 500 home runs and possibly the Hall of Fame. Figure 3.6 shows a hitter using a tap.

Stride Length

The average stride length in the major leagues is 15.17 inches (figure 3.7, p. 40). A hitter doesn't have to take a 15-inch stride to be balanced and under control; the hitter's stride should fit his body type. Good rhythm and the use of an appropriate trigger will take a hitter into his stride.

Striding way over the norm can cause problems such as excessive head movement and late timing. The longer the stride, the more the head drops and the longer it'll take for the hitter's stride foot to land, upsetting his timing. A hitter who takes a very long stride puts himself closer to the ball, decreasing the amount of time he has to react to the pitch.

FIGURE 3.6

Some hitters prefer to use the tap instead of the kick or traditional stride.

The hitter taps back to load while maintaining balance.

FIGURE 3.6 *(continued)*

The hitter tries to stride to balance but has too much weight on his back leg.

The bat is over his shoulder as he is almost balanced.

FIGURE 3.7   This computer-generated drawing of a left-handed batter shows a proper stride length. The average stride length for a major league hitter is 15.17 inches, but the hitter's stride should fit his body type.

Long strides don't lead to more power. Any hitter—whether a contact hitter or a power hitter—will suffer if his stride doesn't fit his body type and if he moves his head excessively on approach. On the other hand, a hitter whose stride is too short can also be in jeopardy if his balance point is not intact.

DANCING WITH THE PITCHER

Timing is really dancing with the pitcher because you must react to his movements. A hitter must put himself in the right position to hit at the right time.

Early timing is better than late timing. If a hitter starts a little too early, he can always slow down and be right on any pitch he recognizes correctly. On the other hand, if a hitter starts too late he cannot make up lost time and will probably rush or jump at the ball.

Whatever trigger or setup a hitter uses to get ready to hit is unique to the hitter—what is not unique is that he must get there on time. Usually when the pitcher breaks his hands to deliver the ball, from the stretch or windup, the hitter must already be in his getting-ready-to-hit motion. A hitter who uses a high leg kick will have to start even earlier than normal.

Once in motion, the hitter's eyes will tell him when and where to deliver the bat. If the hitter starts his ready motion late, he cuts down the time his eyes have to make a good judgment on where and when to deliver the bat and ends up using a very rushed movement.

To time a pitcher, a hitter must trust his eyes and know and feel what he's looking at when he steps into the batter's box. After a pitch or two, a hitter should know if he's close to being on time or if he's too late or too early. It does not matter what pitch the pitcher throws because a hitter must always be on time for the pitcher's fastest pitch. Once the ball is released, a hitter who is on time for the pitcher's fastest pitch can make an adjustment to an off-speed pitch by simply slowing down for a split second and letting the ball travel to the hitting zone somewhere over the plate.

For a hitter, good rhythm and timing require moving in relation to the pitcher's motions. Most of the time, you want to start moving when the pitcher breaks his hands. Whether the pitcher works from the windup or the stretch, he will have to break his hands. He can't fool you. What you're doing is dancing with the pitcher.

When the pitcher breaks his hands, the hitter must maintain his posture and stride on time, landing on the inside of the balls of his feet. The front foot can land open, at almost a 45-degree angle. A hitter should not land on his heels.

A good hitter starts early and slow and maintains a fluid motion. Just keep the motion going until your stride foot lands on the ground. You cannot get aggressive until your foot lands. Many hitters try to get aggressive before they land, turning their approach into a jump or lunge.

Starting your motion early is better than starting late. When a hitter starts early, it's much easier for him to adjust. A hitter can always slow down. A hitter who starts late can never catch up. If you start your motion too early, just say to yourself, "Oh, no, this is too soon," and slow everything down to a fluid movement. Don't stop. If you stop, you'll have to restart. In high school physics, we learn that a body in motion tends to stay in motion and a body that's stopped tends to stay stopped. That's the principle of inertia. This is particularly true when it comes to hitting. Try to keep a fluid motion going all the way to foot landing (figure 3.8).

FIGURE 3.8

a

b

Don't stop in your motion. Your motion from first movement to foot landing should be fluid.

Two eyes focused on the pitch.

FIGURE 3.8   *(continued)*

While striding to balance, the eyes are level.

The front foot opens slightly.

Traditionally, hitters who chased bad pitches were often told to see the ball first, then react. Today, however, this old teaching doesn't hold water. The big problem with this idea is that the hitter will run out of time. The two-tenths of a second the hitter has to make a good decision will be gone.

Seeing the ball is a good idea, but the hitter must see the ball while he's in motion or while he's getting ready to attack. Starting early means that the hitter's body is in motion and is set up to hit the pitch before the pitcher gets to his release point.

Don't be afraid of movement. Timing requires movement. The swing requires movement. Everything about hitting consists of good, strong movements.

Preparation can help a hitter make a better educated plan about what pitches he will look for and what location the pitcher usually likes. This comes from watching the pitcher work to other hitters. What does the pitcher like to do against left-handed hitters? right-handed hitters? What does the pitcher like to do to put away the hitter when there are two strikes? These things are easy to see if a hitter pays attention to the game and what's really going on right in front of him. Look for it, get it, and attack it!

CHAPTER 4

Balance

Hitting consists of four absolutes: *dynamic balance, sequential rotation, axis of rotation,* and *bat lag.* Dynamic balance means the hitter needs to know and control his center of gravity from start to finish. A hitter can control his center of gravity by striding to balance.

By controlling his center of gravity, a hitter can focus his entire body on performing a certain task, such as swinging a bat. Think of the belly button as the center or core of the body. The upper body must be coordinated with the lower body to create energy and speed. (We will discuss this in more detail in the chapter on rotation.) The performance of any athletic movement, especially hitting a moving baseball, requires excellent coordination of the upper and lower body.

Energy starts at the feet and works its way up through the body to the hands and bat to create an explosion between the bat and ball. The old saying, "You're only as strong as your weakest link," still holds true today. Bat speed and quickness increase when the body works in the correct order and all the muscle groups work in sync with each other. Maintaining balance by controlling the center of gravity is essential to making the body perform efficiently. To stabilize the body, try to keep the head over the belly button when executing a high-speed swing at a baseball.

CONTROLLING CENTER OF GRAVITY

To control the body to do a difficult and aggressive movement such as a swing, simply control the body's center of gravity from the start of the swing to the finish.

During the stride, the hitter's posture remains upright with his head directly over his belly button (figures 4.1 and 4.2). The stride foot lands slightly open, meaning the lead foot is at about a 45-degree angle toward the field, with the weight on the inside of the ball of the foot. At this point, the hitter is in his strongest balanced position and is ready to begin a violent rotational movement.

Getting away from a good center of gravity can cause a lot of problems. If you bend way over to swing at a low pitch or collapse over a bent front leg to reach for a pitch out in front of home plate, you risk losing your posture and therefore being unable to complete an effective swing. Both of these problems, and many others, can be controlled by having a great balance point or a strong center of gravity.

Proper posture is a must. Keep your head over your belly button. This will allow you to execute a violent swing while maintaining control. Unlike the trigger, posture doesn't change according to hitting style. Posture doesn't change even when bunting. A hitter doesn't bend over to hit a low pitch or to bunt. Instead, he lowers his body with his legs and keeps his head somewhat over his center of gravity.

FIGURE 4.1   Proper posture is essential for successful hitting.

FIGURE 4.2

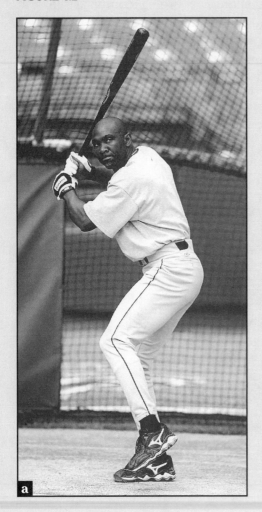

Dynamic balance.

Maintain posture and balance before forward movement.

FIGURE 4.2   *(continued)*

Two eyes on ball; posture is still intact as the front leg starts down.

Rotation begins.

Each individual hitter will choose whether to stand up or crouch down in his stance (figure 4.3). Hitters who crouch must remember to maintain good posture, with the belly button (center of gravity) in line with and underneath the head. A hitter can crouch if he can flex his legs, letting his legs take him lower. A crouching hitter should not bend at the waist, which would cause his head to move away from his center of gravity. If you decide to crouch, it is better to go straight down by bending your legs, not your waist.

FIGURE 4.3   Some hitters prefer to stand straight at the plate; others prefer to crouch.

STRIDING TO BALANCE

Balance means having a strong base on which you can rotate (swing) efficiently at a high rate of speed. Without balance, an athlete will have problems with any activity. That is why dynamic balance is an absolute in hitting.

What we have to understand is how to get to that point. When you step in the batter's box and prepare to swing, you must become dynamically balanced. It's easy to start balanced, then fall to your heels or get on your toes and lose your posture during the swing. Remember, dynamic balance means keeping your balance from start to finish. You start on the balls of your feet, and when you swing, you stay balanced until the swing is complete. That's dynamic balance.

A hitter's goal is to stride to balance. This means that when your stride foot lands, your weight is distributed evenly on the balls of both feet. A hitter is at his strongest hitting position with a 50/50 weight distribution. Not 60/40. Not 70/30. This even weight distribution allows the hitter to move into rotation at the highest possible speed. Keep that balance all the way through the violent action of the swing. Give yourself the best shot at succeeding.

When a hitter strides to balance, he lands on his lead foot, ending his stride and stopping his forward movement. He is then in the strongest possible position to execute a forceful swing. Taking a stride with most of the weight on the back leg leads to a jump or leap off the back side to get at the ball with a swing. Taking a stride and having most of the weight on the front leg leads to poor posture (a lean) and swinging over a soft front leg.

When the stride foot lands, the hitter should be in the athletic position—knees slightly flexed with the head over the belly button. From this position, the body can work efficiently to create bat speed.

Chipper Jones has a great stride to balance, and he uses his tap to get there. No matter how unique a hitter's style is, a good hitter is at his strongest base and body position when ready to attack a pitch.

Chipper Jones uses a tap to stride to balance, giving him a strong base from which to attack the pitch.

CATCHING UP TO THE BREAKING BALL

When a hitter is out in front of any breaking ball or change-up, he may hear the advice to "stay back." Many young hitters take this literally and end up keeping a lot of weight on their back leg, making them prone to jumping forward off the back leg or getting beat on any decent fastball, or both.

A better choice of words might be to "stay balanced" or "stride to balance." The hitter needs to stay balanced on the balls of his feet from the start of the swing to the finish. From this point, a good, quick, forceful attack on any pitch is possible. A good hitter shifts his weight from the back leg to a firm front leg during a quick and aggressive rotational move. He uses his timing and rhythm to allow him to get to a strong and balanced position as his front foot hits the ground to end the stride.

A hitter starts balanced in his stance, then uses a tap, kick, or traditional stride. He comes back onto his back leg as he strides (figure 4.4).

FIGURE 4.4   Stride to balance.

He takes his stride and comes forward to a strong balanced position. In other words, the hitter starts balanced, becomes off balance when his weight is on his back leg, and comes back to a good balanced position, ready to hit. This is striding to balance. Then and only then can the hitter execute his best possible swing.

If a hitter just stands there in balance and then takes a step forward without a trigger, he could become off balance if he shifts most of his weight to his front leg. Always hit from a point of strong balance. Remember, when you stride and land, that's the strongest position you're going to be in until you make contact with the ball. A good hitter shifts from the ball of his stride foot to the ball of his back foot during his approach.

At foot landing, the hitter is in attack mode, ready to take the bat to the ball and through the ball. Remember, when your stride foot lands, that's as far forward as you want to go during the swing. That's when rotation begins.

CHAPTER 5

Recognition

ven if you had John Olerud's swing, you wouldn't be very successful without good perceptual skills. Recognition is a huge key to becoming a good hitter. A hitter who sets up at the right time to hit is ready to pull the trigger when he recognizes the pitch. Recognition means he has to decide what the pitch is, where it is, and how fast it's coming so he can get the bat head to the ball and drive through it at the right moment. After the setup, recognition of the pitch is the hitter's next important task.

Recognition is the most difficult skill for a hitter to learn, and it takes the most time to master. Even major league players have trouble recognizing pitches. When a successful hitter returns to the dugout and a teammate asks what the pitch he hit was, often the hitter won't even know. Usually he'll reply, "Oh, it was a hanger or something." He just recognized a good pitch to hit and hit it.

DEVELOPING RECOGNITION

Learning to recognize the pitch comes only from experience. The more pitches a hitter sees, the better his chances of recognizing a pitch correctly. The pitcher's job is to make it difficult for the hitter to recognize pitches by changing speeds, using deception, and changing cadence with his motion.

The split-fingered pitch is a good example of how pitchers try to upset the hitter's recognition. A split is the most difficult pitch for a hitter to recognize. When it leaves the pitcher's hand, it looks like a fastball, but it dives down out of the strike zone as it nears the plate. The hitter reads "fastball" and swings at a fastball that isn't there.

Players in Little League or Pony League won't have to deal with moving cutters or splits. However, they must deal with centering the ball on the sweet part of the bat. They also must recognize where the ball will be and when it will get there, no matter how fast or slow the pitch. So even though young players don't have to recognize splits or sliders yet, they do have to determine where the sweet part of the bat is in relation to their hands.

Recognition at this level (7 to 10 years old) is a key phase in a young hitter's life. To adjust to certain pitches, a hitter is going to have to move the bat head to where the pitch is going to be within a few tenths of a second. Knowing where and when to place the bat head on a pitched ball is a difficult task that a young player must practice over and over again.

Coaches tend to gloss over recognition and deal more with the mechanics of the swing. Timing, recognition, and a strong mental approach are just as important as the swing itself. A player will have time to develop good recognition skills if he stays with the game and plays every chance he gets. The more pitches a youngster can see, the better his chances of recognizing correctly. Being on time, having two eyes on the ball, and keeping a balanced position will enhance the development of these skills.

Recognizing the pitch while in motion leads to better decisions. Don't be afraid of movement. The stride has movement. The swing has movement. Movement is what drives the ball when it leaves your bat.

A hitter's head will move twice before contact is made with the ball. The first movement occurs during the stride. The second occurs during the swing. In the major leagues, the average head movement during the stride is around 9 inches (figure 5.1).

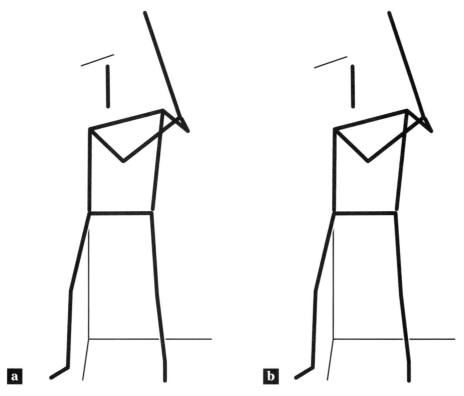

FIGURE 5.1 The average head movement during the stride is 9 inches; during the swing, it's 3.5 inches. Figure *a* shows good posture, with the head up and the hitter ready to begin his movements.

Recognition Problems

I remember a television show long ago that featured Mickey Mantle talking about hitting. He told a story about his best buddy, Whitey Ford, a great pitcher with the New York Yankees. Mickey used to talk to Whitey about hitting all the time. One game, after Mickey had just struck out for the second or third time, he came back to the bench and asked Whitey, "What do you see? Am I doing anything wrong?" Whitey, straight-faced, said, "Mick, looks to me like you're closing your eyes just before you lunge."

A lot of hitters can relate to Mickey's story. Sometimes a hitter feels like his eyes are closed while he's lunging. This usually occurs when the hitter is not on time and everything looks very fast to him. If a hitter doesn't recognize the pitch, he has no chance of hitting the ball.

The hitter needs to keep his head and eyes parallel to the ground during the stride so that he can recognize the pitch correctly. Striding with a downward tilt of the head distorts recognition of the pitch.

In the major leagues, the average movement during the swing is 3.5 inches. A good hitter's head moves less than 9 inches during the stride and less than an inch during the swing. When the head is stable—strong without much movement—the hitter will have his best chance of recognizing and attacking the pitch. It's important to stabilize the head during the swing so that the body can rotate underneath as the hitter correctly recognizes the pitch. Head movement during the swing is a very important part of a good, aggressive swing. The more stabilized the head, the faster the body will rotate sequentially.

STANDING IN

A hitter can do certain things to make it easier to recognize all kinds of pitches. In professional, college, high school, and even some Little League ball, pitchers will perform on-the-side practice sessions to get ready for their next game. This on-the-side work consists of throwing off a mound for 10 to 12 minutes, working all their pitches.

If you see a pitcher performing on-the-side work, get a helmet and bat and stand in to time and recognize all the pitches that the pitcher throws during that session. Stand in just as if you were hitting (figure 5.2). Usually, the pitcher also benefits by having a body in the batter's box. It makes the pitcher's practice more realistic and gamelike. Do not swing. All you want to do is get your timing down. Start early, landing on the inside of the ball of your stride foot. See the ball way out there so you can time it right into the strike zone.

FIGURE 5.2 Stand in when a pitcher is practicing. It helps the pitcher by making his practice more gamelike, and you can work on timing.

Try to track the ball all the way to home plate. You'll lose sight of the ball 8 to 10 feet away from the plate and won't be able to see it again until either it has left your bat or the catcher catches it. Your eyes just aren't fast enough to follow the ball all the way to the bat when you're swinging at high speed.

Standing in against a pitcher who is practicing is something we do in the major leagues, and it really helps with recognition and timing. Stand in against a pitcher any chance you get. It's a simple way to gain experience and learn how the ball moves and breaks as it nears home plate.

Tip: You hit what you see, not what's thrown.

As Ted Williams often said, the most important thing a hitter can do is to get a good pitch to hit. Often a hitter will have to look for a certain pitch. A hitter should be prepared with some knowledge of what the pitcher throws. A hitter also should know his own strengths and weaknesses because it's not very smart to look for a pitch that you can't handle well. When taking batting practice and swinging at all areas of the strike zone, a hitter should take note of which pitches he hits harder and which pitches he hits farther.

Only by taking many, many swings can you find out your strongest area of the strike zone. Most good hitters can handle a few different areas of the strike zone well. Few, if any, can handle all areas of the strike zone.

Use your smarts when looking for a pitch. Remember that if the pitcher throws a pitch you are not looking for, take it! Really good hitters with some experience can look for a certain pitch and still attack a bad breaking ball or a high change-up and be successful. While you are learning, it's better to take those pitches and wait until you get a pitch you can drive. Learn to recognize mistakes even when looking for one certain pitch.

BIG TO LITTLE

A hitter requires his eyes to focus hard on a moving baseball. His concentration level must be high. The problem is that the eyes can focus hard for only a short time before the whole picture becomes distorted. Keeping your eyes relaxed is important.

Information about how to recognize a pitch and then hit it is lacking in the world of baseball. We need more information about how the eyes actually work, as well as the best way for a hitter to focus and see the ball clearly as it approaches the hitting zone. Until we add to our volume of information, you'll hear catchphrases such as hard and soft focus, big to little, and so on.

I like the big-to-little approach, as it seems to relax the eyes. The eyes must be relaxed to see correctly, and that relates directly to the hitter's attitude. A confident hitter who believes he can hit any pitcher at any time probably sees the ball better than a hitter who is not quite sure if he's going to make contact or strike out.

One thing you can do to relax your eyes is to look big and then come back to little. A hitter can look at the outfielders or in the gaps to see where the defense is playing him. He should look away only for a split second, then return his eyes to the pitcher's arm slot (release point; figure 5.3).

I was taught to look at the logo on the pitcher's hat and then move my eyes over to his arm slot and release point. The problem with that tactic is that both objects are about the same size. By looking at two objects of the same size, we defeat our goal of relaxing the eyes. For better recognition, relax your eyes and look at something big first. Then zone in on the pitcher's arm slot and release point and really concentrate on picking up the pitch.

A hitter usually will not be able to see the ball coming out of the pitcher's hand. Good pitchers who have good arm speed make it difficult for a hitter to see the pitch out of the hand because the pitcher's arm moves so fast. If the hitter can pick up the pitch within the first 4 or 5 feet after the pitcher releases it, the ball will look bigger and slower. If the hitter doesn't pick it up until later, the ball is going to look very quick and very small.

Looking at something big and broad, such as the fielders in the outfield, while in the batter's box can help relax the eyes. While in the batter's box, take a second or two to look around and see where an outfielder or infielder might be playing you. Then focus back on the pitcher's release point. This can help make the ball look bigger and slower. Looking at something small such as the pitcher's cap logo before shifting focus to the release point can make it more difficult to pick up the ball, since the logo and ball are about the same size.

Tip: Try to keep your eyes relaxed. Don't put added stress on them by being bug-eyed.

FIGURE 5.3   Looking big to little means focusing the eyes on the outfield (big),
then coming back to the pitcher's arm slot (little).

Squinting a little instead of looking wide-eyed or bug-eyed can help relax the eyes (figure 5.4). Squinting puts less undo stress on the eyes. The eyes work best when they are relaxed and focused on one task at a time.

Imagine being in a poorly lit room and trying to read a sign on the wall. You would probably squint a little so you could focus on the letters. If you look at good hitters such as John Olerud or Mike Piazza, you'll notice that their eyes are almost squinting as the pitch travels from the pitcher's release point to home plate.

Other hitters keep their eyes wide open and bulging out. This stresses their eyes, and they won't see the pitch the way they should. A hitter has only a certain amount of time to focus on his task, and he must take full advantage of it and be as relaxed as possible. Remember that being relaxed doesn't mean you can't be aggressive and in attack mode at the plate. You *can* be aggressive, and you should be.

FIGURE 5.4   Keep your eyes relaxed as you focus on the pitcher.

Recognition will be the last and most difficult skill for a hitter to learn. Recognition comes from experience and seeing enough different pitches to make a good judgment on what the pitch actually is and where it will be in the strike zone.

RECOGNITION AT GAME TIME

While waiting on deck, try to time the pitch. Visualize the types of pitches the pitcher throws (a change-up, a big curve ball, a good fastball, etc.). If you have an idea as to what the pitcher features, you will be ready for any pitch.

In the batter's box, keep your head and eyes stable. Your posture should be strong. Your eyes should stay level to the ground as you take your approach. You try to recognize the pitch. To get the best possible view of the ball, it is best to have both eyes on the pitcher and his release point. Keep your eyes parallel to the ground during your approach. You should not start out as a 6-foot 2-inch hitter and end up as a 5-foot 9-inch hitter because of a severe downward head movement.

A good hitter gets into an early rhythm. This gives him a split second longer to recognize the pitch, leading him to make better decisions and attack only strikes.

Recognition occurs while the hitter is in motion. This is a key point. You cannot be afraid of movement. Moving in a slow rhythm is more efficient than jumping and lunging at pitches. We know this because scientific measurements taken by Bio-Kinetics show that the head does move during the stride and again during the swing. Normally, the head moves 8 to 10 inches during the stride and 3 to 4 inches during the swing. These movements are acceptable as long as the hitter's posture stays intact. Because of the time factor, the hitter has to see and recognize the pitch as he's getting ready. He has only a few tenths of a second before the ball is on top of the plate and he has to attack.

One small thing that helps hitters recognize pitches is anticipating strikes. You don't have time to wait, see what kind of pitch it is, and then say to yourself, "Okay, it's a fastball away. I'm going to hit it." You have to anticipate that the ball is going to be in the strike zone and therefore you're going to swing on this pitch. Say to yourself, "I'm going to swing. No doubt. He's coming to me. Let's go." The only thing that should stop your swing is if the ball is not in the strike zone or if it isn't where you want it to be.

You have to anticipate that it's going to be a strike. You cannot wait to see the ball first and then react to it. That's old school. Many hitters are called guess hitters because they try to guess what pitch will be thrown and attack it with their best swing. A guess hitter is actually one who anticipates a certain pitch but reacts to any other pitch if the pitcher makes a mistake and leaves the ball up or in the middle of the plate. A hitter who anticipates fastball and times a fastball can still attack a bad or hanging breaking ball.

© Jennifer Smith

While waiting on deck for his turn at the plate, a batter should time pitches and note what the pitcher is featuring.

Clear your mind of all outside thoughts. Think *this pitch, this moment*. As I discussed in chapter 2, it doesn't matter if the bases are loaded in the bottom of the ninth and you have a full count. A hitter must be able to clear his mind and recognize correctly. This pitch, this moment has to be a part of your game plan and in your mind at all times.

Recognition leads to good decisions. The better a hitter's pitch recognition, the better decisions he's going to make as to which pitches to attack—he'll attack only strikes. When you see a hitter swing at a slider in the dirt or a pitch over his head, believe me, he wasn't trying to hit that bouncing slider or that pitch up high. He was trying to hit a pitch that for a split second he thought was going to be a strike over the plate. The more time a hitter has to recognize the pitch, the better his eyes will work, resulting in better decisions. The saying "see the ball, hit the ball" has been around baseball for years. It is the simplest of all instructions, but good hitters want better information.

Two-Strike Hitting

The Major League average in 2002 with two strikes was .187. When hitters were 0-2, the Major League average was only .159; when 1-2, it was .172; when 2-2, it was .189; and when 3-2, it was .226. What does this say about hitting with two strikes?

First, don't get into a two-strike count. But since you probably will at some point, let's discuss how to deal with it successfully.

Traditionally, hitters have been taught to change their swings when they have two strikes. Suggestions such as choking up on the bat, widening out with no stride, moving closer to the plate, or crouching down to make the strike zone smaller are common. If a hitter thinks he can hit better doing some or all of these things, then he should hit that way every single time. The real culprit in the low average on a two-strike count is the mind.

Taking charge of the strike zone and concentrating help take away the fear of two-strike hitting. First of all, a hitter knows he has two strikes, so it shouldn't surprise him that the pitcher might try to make him chase a pitch out of the zone or try to paint a pitch on one of the corners, usually the outside corner. Know where the plate is and compete with a clear mind, not one that's thinking, "I can't strike out here." Remember that changing stance or grip or other hitting traits changes the perspective of you, the bat, and the ball. You probably have not trained enough with these changes to be successful. I do not like the strategy of changing mechanics with two strikes.

What you can do is change your thinking. The mind should be convinced that it has complete control of the situation—confidence. Look to hit the ball to the opposite gap since most two-strike pitches are on the outer half of the plate. Two-strike hitting is the most difficult of all offensive situations, so have a plan, do not be afraid of striking out, and know the strike zone.

Just for comparison, here are the 2002 Major League averages on other counts:

- when 0-0, the average was .335;
- when 1-0, it was .324;
- when 2-0, it was .339;
- when 3-0, it was .359;
- when 0-1, it was .309;
- when 1-1, it was .320;
- when 2-1, it was .338;
- when 3-1, it was .357.

It's amazing what two strikes can do to the mind of a hitter if the hitter allows it. Chasing a pitch over your head or a pitch bouncing in the dirt with two strikes comes from either a fear of striking out or a complete lack of concentration. If you strike out on a super pitch, just tip your hat to the pitcher—but tell yourself that he can't and won't do that again.

You will be successful with two strikes if you have a clear, confident mind. Having two strikes is nothing to fear. You can be ready for any strike that comes over the plate. Remember—you can hit a mistake any time and in any count.

After the ball is thrown, early identification—recognition—is probably the most important factor in hitting. Remember that you hit what you see, not what is thrown. The eyes will provide most, if not all, of the critical information your body requires to achieve any task. Everything you do in sports begins with what you see and how you perceive what is going on around you. Hitting a moving baseball will be the most difficult task the body is asked to perform.

On average, a thrown baseball takes about four-tenths of a second to travel from release point to contact. A hitter will use up to half that time with the execution of the swing. That leaves two-tenths of a second to recognize the pitch. This data alone should emphasize how important it is to be on time and get the body in the right place at the right moment. Vision techniques can be improved with concentration, a clear and ready mind, and experience.

Depending on the level of play, you probably anticipate a particular pitch based on the count, the situation, the pitcher, and other factors with a good, educated guess. In the major leagues, many pitchers pitch backward. This means that they throw an off-speed pitch in a fastball count such as 2-0, 3-1, 3-0, and so on. In Little League, high school ball, and most college programs, pitchers will do the expected. This means that a hitter can look for and anticipate a fastball in a good fastball count.

Location will vary depending on the pitcher's control and the situation. With a man on second base and no outs, for example, the pitcher will try to prevent the hitter from hitting the ball to the right side of the infield to move the runner to third base. The pitcher probably will bust a right-handed hitter inside to make him pull the ball to the left side of the infield so the runner cannot advance. To a left-handed hitter, he'll tail and spot the ball away so that the hitter cannot pull the ball and move the runner to third base.

It's very important that a hitter learn how to use the correct angles of the bat when hitting. In a situation with a man on second base and no outs, a good hitter can take an inside fastball and shoot it to the right side. A good left-handed hitter can take a pitch away and shoot it up the middle or hook it back to the right side to move a runner to third base.

Successful hitting doesn't always mean having a high batting average or hitting a lot of home runs. A good hitter can take advantage of situations and help his team win.

CHAPTER 6

Rotation

et's review what we've learned so far. You approach each at bat with an attitude and can time the pitch. You move in a good, fluid rhythm with balance. You start the stride early and land on the inside of the ball of your stride foot. You hold the bat somewhere over your shoulder, ready to fire it through the strike zone when your stride foot lands. You anticipate the pitch over the middle of the plate. You can recognize the pitch.

Now it's time to attack the baseball. Attacking means you always take your best swing. I don't want a hitter to try to just put the ball in play and flip it all over the field. As he gets older, he'll find that infielders will catch the ball and throw him out. When a hitter gets to the higher levels of baseball, he must be able to hit the ball harder, get it through the infield quicker, and be able to reach the gaps with some consistency.

Attacking the baseball simply means that a hitter always tries to take his best shot and his best swing at the ball. Develop the mindset that you're going to hit the ball hard every time. This belief in yourself usually leads to success. Attacking doesn't mean swinging out of control and trying to hit every pitch over the fence. A hitter who is out of control will experience loss of balance, poor contact, and subpar results. When you're in attack mode, you'll attack every pitch with your best swing, using your entire body for energy by moving through a good, fluid sequence.

The old saying, "It's not how you do it, but if you do it," is so true when it comes to attacking a moving baseball. Every level, from Little League to the major leagues, has hitters who use different styles, stances, and approaches to hitting a baseball. Hitters are not clones and should be allowed to have their own styles and setups. It doesn't matter how a hitter sets up or what kind of stance he uses as long as it doesn't interfere with the absolutes of hitting.

For example, if a hitter dives in toward the plate to keep his shoulders in and his front landing foot is square or blocked off so he doesn't fly open, he's actually restricting the rotational movement he needs to fire the bat through the hitting zone. A hitter who bends way over and changes his posture gets away from a good axis of rotation, and his sequence will be inefficient. A hitter who spreads way out with his stance may have problems timing pitches and have poor rhythm going into his rotation. Balance, posture, and sequence are so important that the style of a hitter must not interfere with any one of these absolutes.

Having the mindset to attack the baseball means the hitter takes his best swing at every pitch he decides to hit. Even when a hitter is getting out in front and starting to reach for a pitch, he can still continue to fire the bat head through the ball and have success. Too many times hitters just try to put the ball in play and are satisfied with that accomplishment.

Many young hitters are afraid of striking out, so putting the ball in play is their only goal. Good hitters go to the next level and try to put the ball in play hard and drive it to all parts of the field. That is attacking the baseball.

AXIS OF ROTATION

The axis of rotation is an imaginary vertical line around which the body rotates during the swing. This line passes through the hitter's head and the center of gravity (belly button) and intersects the base of support at a point midway between the feet.

Axis of rotation is important because to create energy from the feet to the fingertips and from the fingertips to the bat, the body must be in a position to deliver that energy. A severe posture change makes it difficult for the hitter to use his entire body to create energy and bat speed.

Imagine a pole going from the top of the hitter's head down through his belly button and splitting both legs (figure 6.1). A hitter rotates around that imaginary pole at a high rate of speed. The straighter and stronger his posture around the axis of rotation, the faster and quicker he can swing. When the hitter involves his hands and bat last during the swing, he has a split second longer to make a good decision as to whether or not to attack.

Hitters who put more weight on their front leg or lean back appear to have their axis out of line. In reality, however, a front-foot hitter just moves his axis forward a few inches but still maintains a strong balance point. Hitters who appear to lean back, such as Barry Bonds, just move the axis back a few inches.

There is no perfect line that splits the hitter. Energy is not lost as long as the body is still in line. Severe posture disintegration—when the head drops, causing a bent-over look—or the hitter's weight falling back on his heels, which causes poor balance, stops energy from going from the ball of the stride foot to the fingertips. Coaches need to realize that some margin of error exists, and hitters will never look

FIGURE 6.1   The axis of rotation.

absolutely perfect. Even major league hitters have differences in style, but these differences must not interfere with keeping the body in line.

A hitter who keeps his head less than 2.5 inches away from the vertical axis and in line with his center of gravity has a greater chance of translating energy correctly at contact (figure 6.2). Taking this energy from his feet to his hands and bat allows the hitter to have efficient bat speed and quickness. The hands will find their own path according to the length of the hitter's arms and his body size.

The closer the hands are to the body, the faster the body can rotate. Also, the closer the head is to a position over the center of gravity—the belly button—the faster the body will rotate. The average major league hitter is 2.1 inches within his vertical axis and in line with his center of gravity.

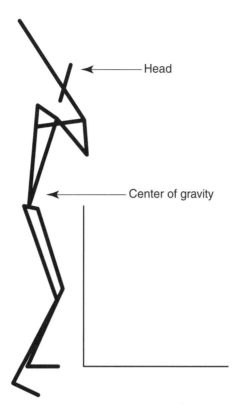

Head

Center of gravity

FIGURE 6.2   Bio-Kinetics data show that a hitter's head should be less than 2.5 inches away from the vertical axis, in line with the center of gravity.

Japanese Hitters

I coached for two years in Japan in both the major and minor leagues, an experience that gave me the chance to see different hitting styles and a different culture's ideas on hitting. Japanese hitters, for the most part, all have a similar style, and many copy their heroes of the past. Sarahara Oh's style, with the hands in front of the face and body, is a popular style. Even his leg kick is copied by many Japanese hitters.

Japanese hitters practice often and take a fantastic amount of batting practice. The problem is that their strength base, their overall strength, is not as high as it should be for a professional ball player to maintain explosion and stamina over a 150 to 160 game schedule.

Weight training is a secondary thought in Japan. Practice time (fielding ground balls, taking batting practice, etc.) is used to gain or build strength. Over a long season, it is

(continued)

difficult to maintain game strength, which is why only a few hitters can come to the United States and succeed. The long season wears down a hitter. Without a good strength base and a good maintenance program, it is difficult for a hitter to play at 100 percent every day.

The hitters in Japan are all in the same boat when it comes to strength, so everyone is on an even playing field. There are a few exceptions, such as Hideki Matsui of the Tokyo Giants, but only a few, and they really stand out as premiere hitters.

Japanese hitters must listen to and obey their coaches. There are some great coaches in Japan, but a lot of coaches come from the "old school" and do not have the most recent information to elevate their players to a higher level of hitting. The coaches I have seen and coached with in Japan really want to learn and become great teachers. All they need is to take the next step and introduce some new ideas to their hitters. If they did this, I'm sure there would be many more hitters ready to play in the United States in the near future.

What happens when a hitter takes a huge number of swings every day is that the hitter will pace himself and not learn to explode through the ball over and over again. A hitter who knows he is going to hit for a long period of time in practice may slow his swing to half or three-quarter speed. Then when he tries to jump to high speed in a game situation, he finds he is in a different timing mode and is not in sync with the pitcher. The explosion won't be there, and the ball will not jump off the bat like it should.

Japanese hitters also are very hands first when it comes to sequence, so power is often lacking. When I coached in Japan, many of the younger players adapted well to using their entire bodies to hit (feet first, hands last) and had good success. But they need someone to keep after them over time to get them to the highest level they can reach. I think with a little help and good information, more hitters from Japan could come to the major leagues in the U.S. and have an impact.

Ichiro Suzuki certainly has had an impact, but he's a special athlete with great natural talent. He has superior speed, an amazing arm, and a tremendous amount of hand–eye coordination. He can put the ball in play from any angle, even as he's on the move out of the box. When I saw him in 1995, he was only 21 years old, and I could tell he would be a star one day. He shows great power in batting practice but chooses not to use that power in a game. Like Wade Boggs and Tony Gwynn, Ichiro could hit a lot of home runs if he wanted to be that type of hitter.

Japanese hitters and coaches are anxious to learn and would work day and night to become better hitters and teachers. All they need is better information, positive reinforcement, and a good functional fitness program.

Some day I would like to return to Japan and reintroduce some of my ideas about hitting to see if I could make a difference. I have borrowed some of their drills and work habits for use in the states, and it seems only fair to return the favor.

Sometimes a hitter who frequently gets jammed or beaten by fastballs is told, "Be quick with your hands." This phrase is meaningless unless the hitter knows how to make his hands quicker. A hitter may try to start his hands forward early to make sure they get into the hitting zone more quickly. This not only takes the hitter out of the correct sequence but actually makes his bat slower.

Getting jammed or being late on fastballs comes from timing, or the position of the ball and bat when the front foot hits the ground. The only way to get into the hitting zone more quickly is to be on time and be aggressive with the lower body.

Quick hands can come only from quick rotation and good timing. Talking so much about the hands will get hitters into more trouble than anything else coaches teach them. Replace "be quick with your hands" with either "start earlier" or "speed up" (the rotation of the lower body). How quickly the lower body rotates determines the bat speed (figure 6.3).

I believe that always talking about quick hands is one of the most harmful things coaches can do to young hitters. It just reinforces the use of the hitter's upper body and gets too far away from the way a hitter should make the bat get through the zone faster—starting with the legs. Emphasizing the hands makes the hitter think his hands must start earlier to get to the ball more quickly. A hitter who hears this advice may

FIGURE 6.3   How quickly the lower body rotates determines the bat speed.

forget about the lower half of his body and try to generate bat speed with his hands.

Hitters have been told to keep their hands back since the beginning of time—get them back, walk away from them, and so on. In actuality, however, the closer your hands are to your center of gravity, the faster you can rotate. The faster the rotation, the faster the bat speed. This is a fact.

Instead of getting your hands back, get them in launch position with the bat somewhere over your shoulder when your stride foot lands (figure 6.4). Your hands will find their own comfort zone during the rhythm and setup. When the hands do get back too far, the swing will look like a cast. This does not allow the bat to come last.

FIGURE 6.4   When the stride foot lands, the hands should be in launch position with the bat over the shoulder.

MOVING ENERGY

Julio Franco was one of the best hitters I ever worked with, an American League batting champion. He displayed the hitter's attitude. He had timing as well as bat speed and bat quickness. He was able to turn potential energy into moving energy.

A hitter who weighs 120 pounds has 120 pounds of potential energy; a hitter who weighs 220 pounds has 220 pounds of potential energy. The trick is to turn that potential energy into moving, usable energy.

A hitter does that by translating energy from the lower half of his body up to his hands and out to the bat head. Simply put, it's feet first, hands last. That's the correct sequence for a hitter. How a hitter moves in sequence is one of the most important factors in how good a hitter he will be—in fact, it may be the most important factor. Remember, a hitter does only two things: he strides and he rotates (swings).

Tip: Linear movement (the stride) must stop before the hitter goes into rotational movement (the swing).

Sometimes a hitter, especially a young one, will add a third movement. After his stride, he will continue to drift over his front leg as he tries to take a good, aggressive swing. A hitter must stop forward movement before he goes into violent rotation.

When a hitter's front foot lands on the ground, the hitter is as far forward as he's going to go during the swing. Rotation begins immediately after the stride foot lands (figure 6.5). Swinging a bat at high speed is a rotational movement. Correct sequential movement of the body creates high bat speed and bat quickness, which translates into a vicious, aggressive swing with force. Let's discuss what correct sequential movement means to a hitter.

When a hitter strides and the stride foot lands on the inside of the ball of the foot, the back heel begins the body's rotational movement. The back heel pops off the ground and starts to turn; rotation begins at that moment.

Tip: A hitter can be as aggressive as his mechanics, strength base, and balance allow.

When you swing aggressively, some people may tell you you're swinging too hard. I think you can be as aggressive as you want to be as long as you keep dynamic balance. A hitter who swings so hard that the force of the swing throws him off balance is swinging too hard. But if you're

FIGURE 6.5   Once the stride foot lands, rotation begins.

swinging as hard as you can and are still able to maintain dynamic balance, with recognition, more power to you. Keep swinging! You've created high bat speed and bat quickness to use in the next split second to attack a moving baseball.

When the stride foot lands, the bat should be over the shoulder. The closer the hitter's hands are to his body, the faster his body will rotate. That concept is based on one of the laws of physics—if your hands are closer to your center of gravity and are not allowed to cast out away from your body, your body will be able to rotate faster (figure 6.6).

During their spins, Olympic figure skaters rotate at a tremendous rate of speed. Sometimes it looks like they're spinning a thousand miles an hour. They rotate so fast you can't recognize their faces. What do these skaters do to achieve that kind of rotational speed? They bring their hands close to their center of gravity, just above the belly button. If they throw their hands out, they'll rotate much slower. A hitter also

FIGURE 6.6   The body will be able to rotate faster if the hands are kept close to the center of gravity.

wants to achieve a high-speed rotation. Therefore, it makes sense for him to hold his hands close to his center of gravity, his core.

A good hitter hits with the lower half of his body first. The bat stays behind, ready to go to the ball and through the ball. The bat is the last link of the swing. This is called *bat lag,* which we'll cover in chapter 8. Remember, feet first, hands last. Energy comes up the legs, through the hips, through the upper part of the torso, through the shoulders, through the arms, to the hands, and finally to the bat head. The hands go to the ball and through the ball.

A hitter's sequence is measured in degrees. The lower body starts the swing (remember, feet first, hands last) and the upper body stays behind. How

Tip: A good hitter doesn't swing down and he doesn't swing up. He always just takes a natural swing through the ball. He does this with a stable posture, keeping his head over his center of gravity.

far the upper body stays behind the lower body tells a hitter how much torque or force he'll have going into contact. In the major leagues, the average hitter's upper body is 25.5 degrees behind his lower body during rotation during the swing (figure 6.7).

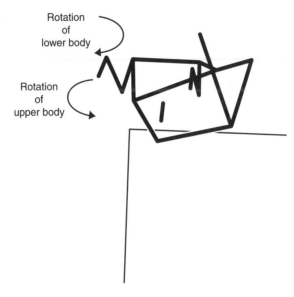

Rotation of lower body

Rotation of upper body

FIGURE 6.7   This overhead view shows the lower half of a left-handed hitter's body leading the upper half of the body during the swing. The difference in degrees between the lower half and the upper half is the kinetic link measurement. The degree to which the hitter's upper body stays behind his lower body determines the force he will be able to produce.

A hitter won't know what kind of torque is being created unless it's measured by a computer during an analysis. A good hitter just has to be ultra-aggressive with his lower body first. The more separation a hitter feels—when the upper body stays behind a little farther and a little longer—the more force will be translated to the final link, the bat. The energy comes up the legs and through the trunk. The belt buckle turns out toward the pitcher, and the upper body whips around. Here's another way to look at it: If you wind a rubber band around your finger a couple of times and then let it go, it unwinds a couple of times and then fizzles out. But if you wrap it around your finger 20 times, it unwinds at a higher speed and creates a lot more force. That's what a hitter tries to do with his body.

The difference in movement between the lower and the upper body is very important. Hitters must master the sequential body movements of hitting. I keep repeating this over and over because it's vital to becoming a good hitter. The order in which the body moves is a major factor in determining how much bat speed the hitter will generate.

Correct sequential rotation of the body is the key to success. Remember: feet first, hands last. Generate power from your legs, bring it up through your torso to your arms, and apply that power to the ball when your bat comes in contact with it.

CHAPTER 7

Front-Side Blocking

Front-side blocking occurs when the front or lead leg snaps straight just before contact with the ball to allow completion of the final link of rotation—the upper body and the bat itself.

When the body stops its forward motion and rotation begins, the front or lead leg snaps straight (gets firm) just before contact. This allows the upper body and the bat to come through the hitting zone at a high speed as the last element of the swing. If the front leg does not snap straight and continues forward with the rest of the body, then bat speed and bat quickness will suffer tremendously. Remember that one body part or muscle group must stop to allow the next body part or muscle group to accelerate.

Front-side blocking simply allows the body to complete rotation in the correct order. Just before the hitter makes contact with the ball, the front leg snaps straight, completing the rotation of the body. Successful hitters always snap the front leg before making contact.

The sequential movements of the body start when the back heel lifts up and the lower body starts taking energy toward the upper body. The legs are slightly flexed as the hips rotate. The hitter's belt buckle almost faces the pitcher. The front leg snaps straight (figure 7.1), finally allowing the upper body and the bat to come flying through the strike zone at a high rate of speed. That's how a hitter's body works to achieve optimal bat speed and quickness. That's the sequence a good hitter follows.

A good hitter is balanced when the stride foot lands. His bat is over his shoulder. His back heel comes off first as rotation begins. The body segments rotate in order, starting with the feet and working all the way up to the last link, the bat itself. When the hitter's torso is fully rotated, his belt buckle turned toward the pitcher, the bat head is still coming from behind the hitter.

As the bat makes contact with the ball, one hand is up and the other is down. The arms are not extended at contact. The contact point is in front of the hitter's body (figure 7.2). The hitter's posture is in line with his axis of rotation, and his head and eyes are stable. The body rotates beneath a stable head. The hitter's eyes look just in front of the contact point.

FIGURE 7.1   The sequential movement of the hitter's body ends when
the front leg snaps straight.

FIGURE 7.2   The hitter makes contact with the ball in front of his body.
His arms are close to his body, and his head and eyes are stable.

Hitters will sometimes hear the advice to "turn on it," meaning to turn on an inside fastball or get the head of the bat out. A hitter who really tries to turn on it will break a lot of bats and hit a lot of foul balls. Neither of these is a desired result.

What the hitter should do is get very aggressive with his rotating lower half. He should move the bat head over so it's at the correct angle on an inside pitch for him to drive through the ball and keep it fair. Moving the bat head over in front of the body at the end of the rotation on inside pitches is more efficient than trying to get the bat head out.

HITTING THE LOW STRIKE

A good hitter always hits against a firm front side, snapping his front leg straight just before contact. Sometimes hitters hear that they should go down and get a low strike. This can cause problems. Going down to get a pitch causes the front leg to collapse. The hitter's posture changes from strong to weak. This change in posture makes his balance and swing less efficient and reduces his hitting success. Once a hitter changes his posture and bends or leans down to get a pitch, two things happen, and neither one is good.

First, bending down takes time, and the ball doesn't stop and wait for the hitter. Even if the extra movement takes only a hundredth of a second, it can alter timing and recognition.

Second, when a hitter leans to get the low pitch, his eyes move closer to the ball. Pitches that are low and away, such as bad sliders and fastballs headed for the dirt, will look like strikes for a split second. As a result, the hitter will chase more bad pitches because his head is closer to the ball. Many hitters will swing at a pitch low and away off the plate because for an instant they think they can hit it. In reality, they can't even reach that pitch, which ends up bouncing in the dirt.

A hitter must keep good posture even on low strikes (figure 7.3). Maintaining good posture with the head over the center of gravity is very important for a hitter to be successful. A hitter who changes his posture to hit different pitches will lose force and energy and is doomed to fail.

It's better for a hitter to recognize a low pitch for a strike and swing at it with the correct mechanics intact. The hitter should keep his eyes parallel to the ground, hold his posture firm, and take his best swing.

FIGURE 7.3   It's important to maintain good posture even when swinging at a low strike.

Inside Pitches

The best player I've seen at hitting a pitch in or up and in is Juan Gonzalez. I coached Juan when he was just a 19-year-old with the Texas Rangers. Juan pulls the bat head through on inside pitches better than anyone, and he has a knack for keeping tough inside pitches fair.

HITTING THE HIGH PITCH

Hitters are taught all the time to chop at the high pitch. The illusion is that the bat head is over the ball (on top). The naked eye thinks it sees a tomahawk or chop swing at the high pitch.

Chopping down on the ball is *not* a good tactic for a hitter to practice or use in a game situation. Remember that as the bat and hands move toward contact, the hands should always be above the ball and the bat head below the ball. On a high pitch, the split second after contact the hitter usually goes into a low finish, which gives the appearance of a tomahawk swing. Some hitters actually will keep going on a high pitch and finish extremely high. The bottom line is that the hands are above the ball at contact, even on pitches up in the zone. The bat path will always be up and through the ball (figure 7.4).

Even major league players can have difficulty reaching the high strike. Bat speed and bat quickness have a lot to do with a hitter's ability to catch up to a high fastball. Take, for example, Pete Incaviglia, who joined the Texas Rangers as a rookie right out of college, where he'd set all the batting records at Oklahoma State University. He was very strong and a pretty decent hitter. Pete had great strength and hit 30 home runs in his first major league season.

Using three-dimensional graphics, digitized images, and motion analysis, Bio-Kinetics overlapped him with Don Mattingly to compare their bat speed and bat quickness. Both hitters had exactly the same bat speed, but not at exactly the same time. Mattingly exploded a little more quickly and got his bat to the hitting zone a bit earlier. Incaviglia's bat head trailed Mattingly's to contact but caught up a few frames after contact. Pete was a little slower through the hitting zone. The result: Pete could not catch up to certain pitches, especially high fastball strikes, despite the fact that he caught up with Mattingly after the bat went through the zone and both finished with the exact same bat speed.

Proper sequencing of the swing increases bat speed and bat quickness. Bat speed and bat quickness are not the same measurements. It's possible for a hitter to have slower bat speed than another hitter but to get to the ball quicker with greater bat quickness.

Bat quickness is measured from the time the bat moves until it makes contact with the ball. Bat quickness could easily be called *quick body rotation,* because the speed with which the body can rotate determines bat quickness. The average bat quickness of a major league hitter is about 0.16 second. That's getting to the ball very quickly.

FIGURE 7.4   When attacking the high pitch, don't chop down at the
ball. Keep your hands above the ball and the bat head below it.

In the major leagues, the average bat speed is about 72 miles an
hour, which gets it through the zone pretty well. You may hear on television that bat speed is 100 to 105 miles an hour, but that just doesn't
happen. The computer measures bat speed in a three-dimensional en-
vironment by time and distance covered.

The loading phase of the swing, or getting ready to hit, is not a factor in determining bat speed. A hitter cannot create bat speed until
both feet are on the ground and the hitter is in a strong, balanced
position. How a hitter gets there is his choice. It's not how you do it,
it's if you do it.

CORRECTING PROBLEMS

When a hitter flies open with the hips too soon in the rotation, his coach may tell him he should stay closed. Staying closed will stop or block rotation. When this happens, the upper body takes over and tries to finish the swing by hooking or rolling over. The front foot lands open on the inside of the ball of the foot.

Staying closed actually means staying balanced on the balls of the feet rather than on the heels. The hands and head do not lead the swing. The hitter's hands will follow his hips. The hips fly open first, and the hands come last. The hands cannot come without the hips opening.

A hitter who overexaggerates his coach's advice to stay back may try to keep his back foot on the ground. However, the back foot needs to release, as its job is to begin rotation. Many hitters have the back foot off the ground at contact or have the toe of the back foot just touching the ground. The weight shift actually takes the weight from the back leg and puts it on a firm front leg with a violent rotational move. Concentrate on a firm front side and let the back foot release.

A coach shouldn't tell his hitters to keep their shoulders level. For one thing, that's an impossible task; one shoulder will always be lower than the other. Dipping occurs when a hitter tries to make contact too deep in the strike zone. If that same swing had a split second longer, it would look like a regular swing. A weak back side can result from a passive first move with the back foot. Instead of the foot aggressively popping off the ground, it rolls over and turns inward.

A hitter can overcome a weak back side and passive first move by knowing and understanding the correct sequence that all good hitters use. Good information and practicing hitting the ball with the lower half of the body, and not just the hands, will help the hitter realize he *must* be aggressive with his legs, and after a short time the move will become natural. Using film, analyzing good information, and working on the correct sequence can help any hitter improve.

Many parents today own video camcorders and tape their children during games and even batting practice. The key to taping a hitter is to

Tip: When you're way out in front of a pitch and out over your front side, you must still keep going and try to finish the swing aggressively. If you slow down the bat to make contact, more often than not you'll roll an easy ground ball to an infielder.

know and understand what to look for while viewing the videotape—first alone, then with the young hitter.

The best angles from which to tape a hitter are straight from the side and straight in from center field. The center-field shot is difficult to get in big parks or stadiums but easy during most Little League games. The side shot shows everything except the timing of the hitter in relation to the pitcher. Using a checklist such as the one shown in figure 7.5 will help you analyze how the hitter performs certain essential elements of the swing.

Look for a loading or timing movement that shows the hitter getting ready to hit. Striding to balance is essential. Next, look at the hitter's foot landing and the position of the bat at that point. See if the lead foot is on the inside of the ball of the foot and open slightly, even to 45 degrees, and see if the bat is over the shoulder. The sequence is now beginning, and the back foot will pop up and begin rotation. This sequence is critical for a young hitter to understand. When the front heel comes down, the back heel comes up. Watch the sequence of rotation as it moves up the body and out to the bat itself.

A hitter can miss the ball and still have a good swing. Make sure a young hitter is aware that hits aren't always the result of a great swing. When a hitter doesn't get a hit, it doesn't always mean he did something

---

What to watch for in a young hitter's swing:

_____ Load and timing movement (stride to balance).

_____ Stride foot lands on inside ball of foot.

_____ Bat is over the shoulder when the stride foot lands.

_____ Back heel comes up when stride foot comes down.

_____ Body rotates from feet to hands and out the bat.

_____ Head stays over the center of gravity throughout the swing.

_____ Posture remains strong.

_____ Firm front leg at contact.

_____ Arms not extended at contact.

_____ High finish.

FIGURE 7.5   A checklist like this one will help you analyze a young hitter's swing.

wrong. Check out the hitter's posture and see if his head made any drastic changes either down or forward. Remember that the hitter must try to keep his head over the belly button all the way through the swing.

When you're watching a tape with a young hitter, pause it at crucial points. Pause it at the moment the hitter's front foot comes off the ground to begin the load and stride. If the pitcher is in the same frame, he should still have the ball at this point. Next, pause the video at foot landing. Where is the bat, and where is the ball? The bat must be over the shoulder and the ball should be about halfway to home plate. Pause the tape again when the back heel begins rotation, and then when the hips are open. Where is the bat head? The bat should be coming last. Go to the moment of contact with the ball and see how flexed the arms are, how firm the front leg is, and how strongly the hitter is holding his posture. The follow-through will be last. Did the hitter finish through the ball, and did he finish high?

Watching a hitter on tape and just looking at results doesn't let the hitter know how he got the hit or why he had such a good (or bad) swing. Try to break down the swing at the key moments and give the hitter the information that will make him a better hitter in the future. Be positive—look for the good stuff first and make corrections as needed. Always remember that if a coach asks a hitter to do something, the next thing out of the coach's mouth should be how and why the hitter's going to do it. A coach who cannot tell a hitter *how* or *why* to do something shouldn't be telling him to do it in the first place!

Have fun with videos, and don't overanalyze. Video can point out some great things, but I've also found that the more a hitter looks at himself on tape when he doesn't quite know what he's looking for, the more things he finds that are wrong. If you look at tape long enough, you'll start to see things that just aren't there. And that can lead to problems.

Watching videotape is a great teaching tool. Use it wisely.

CHAPTER 8

Bat Lag
and Angle

et's review the four absolutes of hitting. Dynamic balance, the first absolute, has to be present from start to finish. The second absolute, sequential rotation, means a hitter rotates his body feet first, hands last. The axis of rotation, the third absolute, is an imaginary line that the body rotates around at high speed.

Bat lag is the fourth absolute. The bat lags behind the body rotation and is the last link in the sequence, giving the hitter a chance to make last-second adjustments to pitches that move, sink, or cut. Because the bat is the last link, the hitter doesn't have to commit as early and won't be fooled as often by off-speed pitches. Contact occurs out in front of the body, not in front of home plate. Contact is the strongest point of the hitter's swing.

When the hitter's hands and bat are in front of his body and are the first to commit, the hitter loses a lot of potential energy. He becomes locked into a certain bat path and will have to stay in that path. If the hands lead the body, he won't be able to make any adjustments.

Hitting a pitch to left, right, or center field is an art that takes a lot of practice to master. In the past, the pitch always determined where it would be hit, and for many batters this is still true. If the ball is away, it is hit to the opposite field; if the ball is in, it is pulled to left field. Today's great hitters, however, can go to the next level and hit most pitches where they want to hit them no matter where in the zone the pitch is thrown. Many good hitters can take a middle-in pitch and slam it into the right center field gap or can take a pitch over the outer half of the plate and slam it into the left center field gap.

Good hitters can do this because they understand how the angles work when attacking a baseball. A pitch right down the middle is contacted by the sweet spot of the bat with the bat below the hands and the hands above the ball. For a right-handed hitter, the palm of his right hand will face up while the palm of his left hand faces down at the contact point (vice versa for a left-handed hitter).

Create correct bat angles with pitches in, out, up, or down. Changing the bat angle will allow you to hit a pitch to any part of the field. This is vital for situational hitting.

A hitter who gets jammed on an inside pitch might hear advice to "get the head out." Getting the head out means throwing the head of the bat out to get to the ball that's coming inside. When the bat head is thrown out, the bat path becomes out to in. The bat path comes around the ball, and the result is often a foul ball, perhaps a long one.

Instead, the hitter must pull the bat head in front of his body so that the head moves over to go through the inside pitch and keep it fair. Changing the angle of the bat near the end of rotation is all the hitter needs to do. Throwing the bat head out leads to top-hand dominance, and the result is a hooking swing. Always take two hands to the ball and through the ball.

BAT ANGLES

Now is the time to understand bat angles and how to hit the ball to all fields. How do you hit a baseball to a certain area of a baseball field? A good hitter changes the angle of the bat. If the pitch is inside, he doesn't need to throw the head out. A good hitter just moves the bat head over and continues on with rotation until he makes contact with the ball (figure 8.1).

To hit an inside pitch and keep it fair, the batter needs to move the sweet spot of the bat only a few inches toward the inside corner. This is done simply by pulling both hands across the body, just enough to get the sweet spot of the bat to the pitch. If the bat comes last in the sequence of the swing, the way it should, then the batter can execute this adjustment in reaction to an inside pitch. Moving the sweet spot over is just a continuation of a good swing that is heading to the middle of the plate. The bat is simply moved over to the inside of the plate when the batter recognizes the inside pitch.

If you have good posture and good balance, moving the bat head over only a few inches will make the inside pitch much easier to attack and keep fair. Hitters who throw the head out instead of pulling their hands in use a lot of the top hand and hit a lot of foul balls. To a pitcher, a long foul ball is nothing but a strike.

The pitchers for the Atlanta Braves make their living on the outside corner of the plate. They will work even farther off the plate if the hitter starts getting close to the right contact point for the pitch. Hitting the outside pitch also requires a continuation of a good swing that is heading for the middle of the plate, only the batter needs to recognize the outside pitch early enough to let the ball travel a little deeper into the zone before making good, solid contact. The sweet spot of the bat will then go to and through the ball if it's on the plate.

FIGURE 8.1   When hitting an inside pitch, a good hitter doesn't throw the bat head out. He simply changes the angle of the bat.

Hitting a high pitch is difficult because of the strength factor involved with a pitch up in the zone. Making solid contact with the high pitch requires a lot of strength, but the principle for using bat angle is the same as with hitting any other pitch.

If the pitch is high, you don't need to chop the ball. A good hitter will just throw both hands to the ball and through the ball (figure 8.2). Always keep your hands over the ball and the bat head below your hands. This is the natural path of a bat accelerating through the strike zone at high speed. The hitter can't stop it.

FIGURE 8.2   On a high pitch, throw your hands to the ball and through the ball. Your hands should be over the ball, and the bat head should be below your hands.

To hit the high pitch, the batter again keeps the bat below his hands and keeps his hands above the ball at contact. Hitting the high pitch will be more difficult because the hands must get over the ball, and that takes strength and speed.

The old "high, hard one" is still the most difficult pitch to hit if it's thrown with good velocity. On the other hand, a high breaking ball should be crushed because the hitter has a little more time to get the bat and hands in the right spot for contact.

Hitting a low pitch requires the same swing as hitting a pitch down the middle. The hitter must maintain good posture and not break down to go get the pitch.

Pitches low and away and up and in are even more difficult because they take a little longer to get to. Timing and recognition have to be top-notch for the hitter to have any consistent success against pitches low and away or up and in. Experience and dedicated practice are needed to achieve mastery of timing and recognition. (See chapter 3 for more about timing and chapter 5 for more on recognition.)

The key to hitting any pitch is to use the correct body sequence to allow the bat to come last. The hitter doesn't have to swing down at a low pitch or up at a high pitch. A hitter only needs to swing through the ball with both hands, make bat angle adjustments in reaction to the pitch, and everything else will take care of itself.

A hitter who hits a lot of fly balls may be advised to "get on top." The problem occurs when a hitter tries to get on top of the pitch with the bat head. When a hitter tries to get on top, the first movement with his hands will be upward. This puts the hitter out of sequence (feet first, hands last) and changes his timing, which will lead to failure. This never happens during a full swing; in fact, it's not possible. To get on top of the pitch, the hitter's hands—not the bat head—should be over the ball. That's getting on top. The hitter must get the hands over the ball and finish high.

The proof of a good swing, regardless of the pitch location, is that the front leg snaps straight right before contact. At contact, the hitter's eyes look out front, not down at home plate. His head is in a strong position, his eyes look toward the release point, his body rotates, and he finishes high. These are the things all good hitters do.

BAT LAG

Taking the knob of the bat to the ball (figure 8.3) has been part of hitting instruction for many years. As a player, I was taught to take the knob to the ball, and it's still being taught today. A hitter who takes the

FIGURE 8.3   Many coaches teach hitters to take the knob to the ball. This is consistent with the fourth absolute of hitting—bat lag—but must be taught with caution.

knob to the ball, or stays inside the ball, is employing one of the absolutes of hitting—bat lag. The feeling a hitter gets by taking the knob to the ball is that of the bat lagging behind. Teaching a player to take the knob to the ball is an attempt to eliminate casting, or letting the hands get too far away from the body, which slows rotation.

A hitter must be careful not to allow his bottom hand to push toward the ball when he tries to take the knob to a pitch. A hitter who creates an extreme angle with too much bottom hand going to the ball will lose power and will find himself hitting too many opposite-field pop-ups.

Coaches should be careful when teaching hitters to take the knob to the ball. Many coaches believe in the concept and teach it daily. They need to be sure, however, that both they and the hitters really understand what is being taught—that the bat will be the last link of the swing, and the arms and hands will be in their strongest position at contact, one palm up and one palm down. If the knob goes directly to the ball, the proper hand position cannot be achieved.

To create a good, strong angle with the bat, one hand must be up and the other must be down at contact (figure 8.4). Taking the knob to the ball puts the hands in a weak position in which both sets of knuckles face up instead of the palms of the hands. The angle of the bat becomes too extreme for good, solid contact.

Fooling the Media

A couple of years ago, John Olerud, one of the purest hitters you'll ever see, was with the Mets. He had been struggling for a few games, so we were in the cage for batting practice. I noticed he was getting an extreme angle with the knob and was flipping balls the other way with nothing behind the swing. I told him to forget taking the knob to the ball and instead to take two hands to and through the ball.

That phrase clicked with John. He immediately felt it and started working on taking two hands to the ball, finishing through the ball, and finishing high. That night he hit a couple of doubles and a home run, and he went on a monthlong hitting terror.

As fate would have it, that night one of the major networks covering the game analyzed John's swing. They concluded that he was such a great hitter because he always took the knob of the bat to the ball—the very movement I took away from him that day in practice. It's funny how sometimes your eyes can see things that aren't really there.

FIGURE 8.4   At contact, one hand is up and the other is down on the bat. This creates a strong angle.

Staying inside the ball actually means letting the bat lag last as the hands direct the bat head to the correct angle for that pitch. An inside-out swing simply pulls the bat head across the body to get it into the correct position to drive the pitch and finish high. This then becomes the last link in the sequence of the swing. Taking two hands to and through the ball is better.

Taking two hands to and through the ball (one palm up and the other down) creates the same feeling without the extreme angles that can occur when a hitter tries to take the knob to the ball. There is also more power and less chance of error.

HITTING THROUGH THE BALL

How should the bat be held? The only thing a hitter doesn't want to do is bury the bat handle deep into his hands (figure 8.5a). Many a bone bruise has resulted from pushing the bat too deep against the thumb of the top hand. A hitter doesn't have to have the bat out toward the ends of his fingers, either, unless he's strong enough to handle it (figure 8.5b). Lining up the knuckles is good in theory, but every hitter's hands are different sizes, and the knuckle alignment may not feel right for everyone. Each hitter should find a grip he feels comfortable with.

The grip should feel comfortable. Keep in mind that you will tighten your grip during the swing. A hitter should experiment with the grip until it feels right. When in doubt, place the bat right in the middle of your hands.

Hitting down through the ball was taught many years ago and is still being taught today. Old-school coaches talk about hitting the bottom half of the ball to get good backspin so it will carry farther. Some coaches admit they know this doesn't happen, but they teach it anyway to correct a hitter who hits too many pop-ups and fly balls.

This idea can be very confusing to a hitter because he can't swing down on the ball, although he can perform the initial move of swinging down. The result is that the rotational sequence goes backward, the opposite of feet first, hands last.

If a hitter is good enough to hit the bottom half of the ball, he might as well hit dead center instead. Advising a hitter to do something that can't happen to get him to do something that should happen is poor teaching. A coach should teach what does happen and make sure the hitter understands what's really going on with his swing. It's better to teach hitters to hit through the ball.

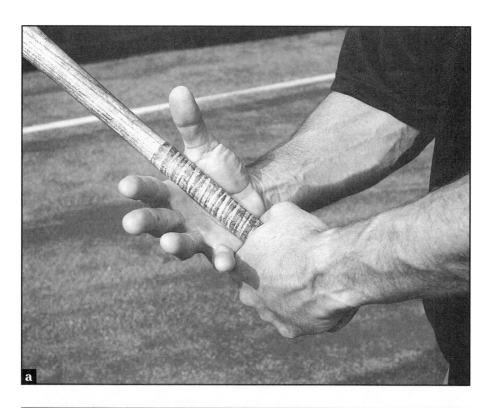

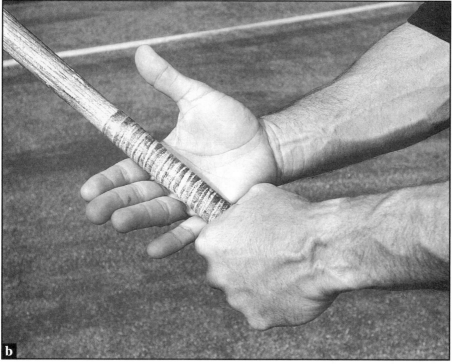

FIGURE 8.5   (a) Don't bury the bat handle too deep against the thumb. (b) Find a grip that feels comfortable for you with the handle more toward the fingers.

CHAPTER 9

High Finish

The high finish is the result of a good bat path. The bat comes through the zone, through the ball, and to a natural high finish. A high finish means finishing the stroke somewhere over the shoulder. A low finish means finishing somewhere below the shoulder. Whenever the bat finishes low, it had to leave the strike zone early just to get to that low finish. Often a hitter who finishes low will miss the opportunity to attack the ball with high force.

After the hitter hits through the ball, he should try to finish high. By finishing high, the hitter keeps the bat in the strike zone longer and cuts down on his margin of error. Contact with the ball is always out in front of the hitter's body, not over the plate, with one hand up and the other down at the contact point.

© Joe Robbins

The batter makes contact with the pitch out in front of his body, not over the plate.

The bat itself will always come at an upward angle toward the pitch. The bat goes to the ball and through the ball at the angle determined by the location of the pitch—high, low, inside, or outside. The hitter must focus on attacking through the ball, realizing that a good high finish is the result of a good swing. Finishing high should not be the focal point of the hitter. Hitting through the ball is the only focal point, and the high finish should happen naturally as the result of a good, aggressive swing through the ball.

A hitter doesn't always know where he'll make contact. By finishing high, he increases his chances for good, solid contact. A good hitter doesn't top-hand the ball (roll over) at contact, nor does he push at the ball (take the knob to the ball) with his bottom hand. Look at a good hitter when he makes contact. You'll see that his arms are not extended, and one hand is up and the other is down as he takes both hands to the ball and through the ball. Good hitters have almost a 90-degree bend in their elbows at contact (figure 9.1).

FIGURE 9.1   A good hitter at contact. Note the bend in the elbows and the position of the hands.

The strongest point of a hitter's swing is at contact. If you put a fairly heavy weight in your hands with your arms in the curl position (90 degrees), you can hold the weight and move it rather easily. If you put the same amount of weight in your hands with your arms extended straight out (180 degrees), you're going to drop it.

When it comes to hitting, almost everyone talks about extension. Sometimes hitters will try to extend their arms at contact, which is not good. At contact, the arms should be flexed (figure 9.2). Extension shouldn't take place until after the ball leaves the bat. Once the hitter has fully extended, rotation decelerates and the bat loses speed. Let the ball come into your contact area and make hard contact with one hand up and the other down and your arms flexed at close to a 90-degree angle, depending on the location of the pitch.

FIGURE 9.2   The arms should be flexed at contact.

Coaches teach extension because when a good hitter finishes high, as he should, it appears that his arms were extended at contact. But they absolutely were not.

Tip: Extension doesn't occur until well after the hitter makes contact with the ball.

Let the ball travel to your contact zone, which is out in front of your body, not out in front of home plate. Hit the ball with one hand up and the other down. Go to the ball and through the ball while finishing high to keep the bat in the strike zone longer (figure 9.3). This is what good hitters do.

FIGURE 9.3   Finishing high will keep the bat in the strike zone longer, increasing your chances of making contact with the ball.

If a hitter finishes his swing low, the bat will go into and out of the strike zone very quickly because it has to leave the strike zone early to get down to a low finish. This decreases the hitter's chances of making contact with the ball.

A unique aspect of some hitters is that they let go of the bat with the top hand during the high finish. The length of a hitter's arms, the tightness of his upper body, and his posture usually will determine if he lets go of the bat or not.

The excuses "he's got a long swing" or "he has a slider-speed bat" cover a lot of mistakes, anywhere from poor timing (being late) to casting the bat out and away from the hitter's center of gravity. The closer the hands are to the body, the quicker the rotation. The quicker the rotation, the quicker the bat speed. Therefore, if the bat casts out and away from the body, it will take longer to get into the hitting zone. The longer the stroke, the slower the bat speed.

To fix these mistakes, first look at timing, and then at the bat position at launch. Both of these factors result in the appearance of a long swing or a swing that never seems to catch up to a decent fastball. Timing is usually the culprit. Simply by starting a little earlier, the hitter will give himself enough time to catch up to more pitches.

The next thing to look at is the hitter's rotational sequence. A long swing is just a swing that takes too much time to get to the hitting zone. Increasing the speed of the bat and getting to the hitting zone more quickly come from good timing and correct rotational sequence.

It takes experience as well as an understanding of the correct mechanics to be able to recognize what a hitter must do to correct a flaw. It's not easy to recognize a hitter's problem right away, and a coach must understand what he's looking at when he watches film or watches a hitter swinging live. In time, it will become easier for the coach, and the hitter will benefit from good instruction.

CONSTRUCTING THE FULL SWING

We have covered a lot of material in this book so far. You now have all the elements of a professional, efficient, major league swing. It's time to review what we've covered and put it all together.

First, timing and rhythm are crucial. You must be in a good, balanced position to hit while the pitch is still far enough away for you to recognize it. Whatever kind of trigger you use—tap, kick, or stride—you have to start it early enough to give yourself as much time as possible to see the pitch (figure 9.4).

FIGURE 9.4   The stride.

Second, you must land on the balls of your feet at the correct time—when the pitch is still about halfway to home plate (figure 9.5). Again, this will give you as much time as possible to recognize the pitch.

FIGURE 9.5   Land on the balls of the feet when the pitch is about halfway to home plate.

Third, recognizing the pitch while you're in motion leads to better decisions (figure 9.6). Don't be afraid of movement. The stride has movement. The swing has movement. Movement is what drives the ball when it leaves your bat.

FIGURE 9.6   Recognize the pitch while moving.

Fourth, correct sequential rotation of the body is the key to success. Remember, feet first, hands last (figure 9.7). Generate power from your legs, bring it up through your torso to your arms, and apply that power to the ball when your bat comes in contact with it.

FIGURE 9.7   Correct sequential rotation: feet first, hands last.

Fifth, contact occurs out in front of the body (figure 9.8), not in front of home plate. Contact is the strongest point of the hitter's swing.

FIGURE 9.8   Contact occurs in front of the body.

Sixth, create correct bat angles with pitches in, out, up, or down (figure 9.9). Changing the bat angle will allow you to hit a pitch to any part of the field. This is vital for situational hitting.

FIGURE 9.9   Create the correct bat angle.

Finally, finish through the ball and finish high (figure 9.10). A high finish keeps the bat in the strike zone longer, increasing a hitter's chances of making solid contact with the ball.

FIGURE 9.10   Finish through the ball and finish high.

Do What Good Hitters Do

Many elements of being a good hitter depend on individual preference, comfort, and what feels good. The only time a hitter must adjust is if his feelings or comfort level hinder the truly important aspects of hitting.

For example, if a hitter's stance is so closed that he can't get into rotation by going feet first, hands last, then he's going to have to make an adjustment. If a hitter is so wide open that he can't cover the outside of the plate because he steps away, then he's going to have to adjust his stance. Experience and good information will help a hitter make these necessary adjustments.

A good hitter

- has dynamic balance from start to finish,
- holds his posture throughout the swing,
- shows sequential rotation (feet first, hands last),
- has a firm front side at contact,
- is strong at contact, and
- finishes high.

If you want to advance to a higher level of play, you need to be clear about what's really important in hitting. Remember what the good hitters do! All good hitters have dynamic balance from start to finish. All good hitters have sequential rotation, which means feet first, hands last. All good hitters have a firm front side that snaps straight just before contact. After a hitter snaps his lead leg straight and makes contact, he can either give and break down or he can stay up with the front leg straight. All good hitters are strongest at contact when the arms are not fully extended. All good hitters finish high.

All these things are very important for a hitter to understand. Younger players, in particular, need to learn and understand these factors to become better hitters. Young hitters often get caught up in individual style rather than the effective movements that create energy and bat speed. Personal style is important, but it shouldn't be the key point coaches teach young hitters.

Some elements of hitting are unique to the style of each individual hitter, such as bat weight, bat length, grip on the bat, stance (opened, closed, or straight), elbow position (up or down), and posture at the plate (standing up straight or crouching down). Young hitters just taking their first steps toward learning how to hit frequently ask about these elements. It's important for coaches to remember that the way a young hitter hits this year will probably change by next year. As the hitter matures, he'll need to make adjustments as he starts settling into the unique style that fits him. I want a hitter to feel comfortable with his own style. The only time he should alter any of his individual style choices is when it interferes with one of the absolutes of hitting.

For example, a coach will want to work with a hitter who dives in toward the plate and changes his posture, as this interferes with the absolute of dynamic balance. Similarly, a hitter who wants to use only his hands to flick the bat head will interfere with the correct sequential movement a hitter needs to be efficient. And a hitter who wants to bend way over to get a better look at the pitch will interfere with the axis he needs to achieve his highest possible bat speed. Unique styles are great, and almost any style can work, but knowing the absolutes and why they are important will help a hitter make a good choice when deciding how he will approach the ball and attack the pitch. It's important to remember that, although there are as many unique swings as there are hitters, hitters look different doing the same thing.

A hitter's preferences regarding bat weight and length are determined by how strong the hitter is at the time. A kid who is a little stronger than most can use a slightly heavier bat. A kid who isn't as strong should use a lighter bat. Major league hitters use bats that weigh 31 to 34 ounces, which isn't that heavy. They choose lighter bats when they want greater bat speed to give them a split second longer to recognize the pitch.

Tip: Pick the bat that fits you. If you have doubts, choose the lighter bat.

An old theory is that the heavier the bat, the farther the ball goes. That's true, but there's a catch. If a heavy bat and a light bat are swung at the same speed, the heavier bat will drive the ball farther. Unfortunately, most hitters aren't able to swing a heavier bat as fast as they can a lighter bat.

The length of the bat it is determined by the length of the hitter's arms and how much of the plate he can cover while swinging the bat. Can a hitter cover both the outer and inner halves of the plate? Experiment with different bat lengths until you find one that fits and feels good.

Should a hitter use an open stance, a closed stance, or a straight stance (figure 9.11)? The choice is unique to each hitter. Some hitters open up a little to get a better look at the pitch. Some like to be closed because they feel that they're stronger and their shoulders and head will stay in longer. As a hitter grows older, he will make several adjustments to move up to the next level, changing his style along the way. It happens to every hitter. A hitter should do what feels good—keeping in mind, of course, the absolutes of hitting.

FIGURE 9.11   Stances: *(a)* open, *(b)* closed, and *(c)* straight.

Should the elbows be up or down during the stance and setup? Young players, eight or nine years old, who are not yet fully developed and have a low strength base will probably have a problem keeping their elbows up all the time. Because their deltoids are not fully developed, the position strains their arms. They shouldn't have to hit from that position. All hitters bury their elbows in their sides on the way to contact and when contact is made. Find a stance that's comfortable and forget about the elbows; they'll automatically go where they're supposed to (figure 9.12).

FIGURE 9.12   Different players use different elbow positions. Find the position that feels the most comfortable.

BUNTING

Although this book focuses on the techniques of the full swing, you shouldn't overlook the importance of bunting to the modern game. An effective bunt at the right time can score a run, move a runner over, or just surprise the defense. A speedy runner who can also bunt consistently can be a devastating addition to the batting lineup.

Baseball is angles, distance, and timing. Bunting successfully, either to move up a runner or to get a base hit, requires skill; mastery of bat angle, ball direction, and distance; proper timing; and the "touch" of bat and ball with eye and hand coordination under pressure. Think "small ball," manufacturing runs with strategy and finesse, not "long ball," scoring runs with brute strength and power. Body mechanics for bunting require the same balance and posture as when completing a full swing. Obviously, the arms and hands will be different.

There are different ways to set up and bunt successfully, but a good bunter must learn and execute specific techniques that will lead to success. There are key techniques in bunting, just as there are in executing a full swing. A good bunter has to get to the proper position and be able to deal with the pressure of the game situation. The speed of the game and the importance of a good bunt become magnified in real time, so the hitter must be prepared with good positioning and a strong commitment to success.

The first key to successful bunting is plate coverage. A hitter should step closer to the plate with his back foot as he squares around. A right-handed hitter squares around as if the second baseman were the pitcher (figure 9.13); a left-handed hitter squares around as if the shortstop were the pitcher. From this position, the hitter can rotate his hips and eyes back to the pitcher while maintaining plate coverage. If the bunter squares around and faces the pitcher, he will not have plate coverage and an outside pitch will seem a mile away.

A bunter can square around one of two ways: the heel-to-toe method or the pivot. A right-hander using the heel-to-toe method squares around by moving his back foot forward (heel) and rotating it (toe). Although this is the easiest position for most bunters, it comes with a built-in fear factor. Many bunters feel that this position doesn't allow them to get out of the way of a pitch thrown up and in.

FIGURE 9.13   A right-handed bunter squares around as if the second baseman were the pitcher.

For the pivot, a right-handed hitter assumes his normal stance, then moves his right foot slightly forward toward the plate and moves his left foot forward and in. This position allows the hitter to react better to a pitch thrown up and in; he can simply turn away from the pitch.

Knowing how to position a bunt according to the game situation is the second key to successful bunting. What type of fielder is the pitcher? the first baseman? the third baseman? Can they cover ground quickly? What does the situation call for? Does the third baseman need to field the bunt so a runner can advance to third?

Get the body into position early for a sacrifice bunt, late when bunting for a base hit. Foot position may vary depending on the hitter and the situation. The feet can remain in traditional batting stance position, the front foot can open up, or the back foot can move ahead of the front foot. The torso and shoulders will always square up with the pitcher before contact with the ball. Body position must allow the bat to contact the ball in front of home plate. The flexion of the knees and the posture of the hip and spine should minimize head or eye movement in any direction but toward the pitcher. Good bunters have quiet heads and hands.

A sacrifice bunt may be called for to advance a runner into scoring position, increase the pressure on the defense, or change the pitcher's approach to the game. There is no surprise when you sacrifice bunt. It is okay to show bunt early, but it is important to bunt at strikes. With a runner on first and no outs, move the ball toward first base. With runners on first and second and no outs, move the ball toward third base. On a squeeze bunt with a runner on third, show bunt late (after the pitcher's front foot lands) and put the ball in play anywhere on the ground.

Bunting for a base hit can be used to take the pitcher out of his game, take the defense out of position, or to change the pitcher's pitch selection. The defense should be surprised when you bunt for a base hit, so show bunt late. Strategically, bunt toward third base when you think the third baseman is playing too far back to field and throw the bunted ball to first base before you get there. Bunt toward first base when you think you can make the first baseman field the ball and then beat him or the pitcher to first base.

When bunting for a base hit, the thought process and execution are the same as when executing a sacrifice bunt. The difference is in the timing and the rhythm relationship with the pitcher. Good timing does not give away the drag bunt, and good rhythm with the pitcher allows the bunter a good head start toward first base. Although deception is good, making a perfect bunt will result in more base hit bunts.

A right-handed hitter who bunts to the right side (a push bunt) should stay higher with his body than when sacrificing and should look for pitches middle away and up. He should preset his bat angle and catch the ball with his bat just as in sacrifice bunting, continuing his movement through the ball in the direction of the bunt. For a right-handed hitter, this bunt can be very effective against a left-handed pitcher who falls off the mound toward third base.

A left-handed hitter who bunts toward first base (a drag bunt) must create more bat by not moving his hands all the way to the label, allowing more of the bat to be used for contact. He presets his bat angle to first base, then catches the ball with the bat, continuing in that direction. With the drag bunt, the bunter must catch the ball on the bat with a continuation toward first base.

The third key is the sitting or bent-knee position. After squaring around, the bunter flexes his knees and crouches so that the bat is set at the top of the strike zone (figure 9.14). This position helps the bunter remember that any pitch above his hands is a ball and should be taken.

FIGURE 9.14   The bunter sets the bat at the top of the strike zone.

Pitches down in the strike zone must be bunted from the squatting position (figure 9.15), which helps maintain plate coverage and keeps the bat-eye relationship steady. On a low pitch, many bunters make the mistake of bending over, changing the relationship of the eyes and bat to the pitch, creating a distorted view of the pitch and making it more difficult to execute a successful bunt.

The fourth key is to get a strike or a good pitch to bunt. Getting a good pitch to hit is essential in full-swing hitting, and it is essential with bunting, although this key does not apply in a squeeze bunt situation. For all other bunts, the bunter must be in good position with good posture and must focus on getting a pitch he can handle. If getting to the pitch requires the bunter to change his posture, the pitch probably will not be a strike.

FIGURE 9.15   To bunt a low pitch, the hitter must bend his knees and lower his body.

The fifth key is to deal with fear. Some bunting positions make the bunter more vulnerable to a pitch thrown at him. It's hard to move out of the way of a pitch when the body is wide open and is a clear target for a pitch in and off the plate. The bunter can alleviate this fear with a good body position and a strong base that allows for quick movement. A good bunter is fearless and must take his nose to the baseball to be successful.

The sixth key is the position of the bat and the bunter's grip. The bat must be out in front of the body with a slight upward angle, and it must cover the entire plate. (If the bunter dropped the bat, it would cover the plate.) The grip must be firm, with the top hand near or on the label. The top hand must be behind the bat to protect it from being hit by the pitch. The bottom hand is used to stabilize the bat and should be placed comfortably between the label and the knob (figure 9.16).

FIGURE 9.16 The top hand is on or near the label; the bottom hand, which stabilizes the bat, is between the label and the knob.

The position of the hands on the bat when bunting—whether for a sacrifice or a base hit—is the same. Position the bat at the top of the strike zone with the bat head above the handle, the top hand balancing the bat in a comfortable grip on or slightly above the trademark, and the bottom hand somewhere below the trademark and above the knob. Set the bat angle in the direction of the bunted ball (figure 9.17). Bat angle is approximately parallel to the first base line for a bunt down the third base line and approximately parallel to the third base line for a bunt down the first base line. For a right-handed batter, a drag bunt goes down the third base line and a push bunt goes down the first base line (the opposite is true for a left-handed batter). The top hand always creates the angle of the bat for placement. If the angle is set correctly, the ball will go where you want it to go.

FIGURE 9.17   The bat angle will determine where the bunted ball goes.

Finally, we get to the bunt itself. A good bunter "catches" the ball on the bat with his top hand. A good drill for practicing this is to wear a glove on the top hand, get into good bunting position, and catch pitches as they are thrown (no bat). Catching the ball with the glove (in front and softly) exactly mimics what the bunter should do when catching the pitch with the bat.

A bunter who has no strikes can be more exact with the direction of the bunt. With one strike, his goal should simply be to deaden the ball anywhere in front of home plate. With two strikes, the bunter has to put the bunt in play and take his chances.

Many bunters are more effective bunting to one side of the field or the other. If this is the case, the bunter should focus on deadening the ball in his strongest direction. In all cases, the bunter must be committed to getting the job done and must want to be successful and not harbor any fear of failure.

Bunting is becoming a lost art because hitters prefer to work on their full-swing hitting rather than their bunting. It's way more fun to watch a ball jump into a gap than to watch it dribble down the third base line. But hitters who are committed to being good bunters can win games; not caring about the little stuff can only lose games.

A successfully executed bunt can be crucial in key game situations. Late in the game and down by more than one run, base runners are a top priority. A bunt for a hit can be more crucial than a solo home run in this situation because a two- or three-run home run isn't possible unless there are runners on base. A good bunter can avoid hitting into a double play, possibly keeping a rally going. A proficient bunter can take the defense out of its normal positioning and comfort zone. Ground balls that would usually be fielded and result in an out can turn into base hits and become opportunities to score runs.

Bunting effectively requires skill and finesse under pressure and is a necessary part of every hitter's arsenal. Obviously, power guys will seldom be asked to bunt, but for every other player on a team (pitcher included), bunting mastery is a must. Hit it, bunt it, score it.

CHAPTER 10

Practice

Practicing what really happens in hitting allows hitters to be as close to game ready as possible. Always try to keep practice work and skill work as close to real time as possible. Having a hitter swing down through the ball so he won't dip or uppercut is poor teaching. Swinging down does not and will never happen. The habits of uppercutting or dipping are not fixed by changing the stance or setup.

Many good hitters have the work habits required to succeed. It's not easy to practice hard every time. It takes a mentally strong and committed athlete to put in the time needed to excel at the next level. The old saying "practice makes perfect" should really be "*perfect* practice makes perfect." Hitting a baseball will never be a perfect skill. Each hitter must realize this and not be devastated by small failures!

Motivation to succeed must come from within, and coaches can only help it along. Being positive and allowing hitters to make mistakes as they learn will motivate most hitters to reach their top potential without fear of failure. Some great hitters are self-motivated. They have that inner strength, and they set goals they can reach. These hitters need the best information possible at their fingertips so that they will propel themselves to the highest levels. Other hitters need to be prodded along and handled with positive reinforcement so as not to disturb their fragile makeup. A good coach will be able to determine the type of hitter he's dealing with if he takes the time to get inside the heads of his students.

Remember that when you tell a hitter to do something, such as hit the ball to the opposite field, the next words from your mouth must be *how* to do it!

Great hitters like Tony Gwynn put in many hours behind the scenes to improve their skills and increase their odds of success. Watching films, studying tendencies, and knowing their own limits can turn good hitters into great hitters. At the major league level, the information at hand is astounding for hitters who want an extra edge when they step into the batter's box.

The amazing thing is that not every player will take advantage of the information available. A good hitter like Julio Franco always wanted to know what the opposing pitcher used to put hitters away. Knowing this gave him a plan when he was behind in the count, and he'd be ready for that time of the at bat.

A lot of coaches in youth leagues, Little League, and high school are clearly overworked and understaffed. Often these teams don't have

Adventures in Spring Training

April Fool's jokes are a common occurrence in Major League spring training camps. One outstanding prank I remember occurred when I was with the Texas Rangers. One spring training day in Port Charlotte, Florida, Bobby Valentine cooked up an April Fool's trick to play on big Larry Parrish. Larry was a great guy, a super hitter, and would later become a manager himself with the Detroit Tigers.

That April 1, Bobby called Larry into his office and told him about a local card shop in Port Charlotte that was really desperate and needed one of the Texas Rangers to come in and sign autographs for a couple of hours to pump up business. He would be paid well for the time, but he had to rush over in full uniform right away so he could get back in time for the rest of the day's workout. Big Larry agreed and borrowed one of the rental cars the coaches used to quickly drive to the little card store in the middle of Port Charlotte. Larry walked in, in full uniform, and announced his presence and that he was ready to sign some autographs. The store owner, in an absolutely empty store, looked at him like he was crazy. Larry immediately knew he was the goat of an April Fool's trick. He drove back to the complex where many of us were waiting out front near the parking lot, anticipating his return.

Larry calmly got out of the car then reached in and put the car in drive. We all watched in shock as the team's rental car started rolling toward the lake that surrounded the Port Charlotte complex. The car took a nosedive into the lake and started to sink. Larry just walked past everyone and went through the clubhouse and onto the field for the workout as if nothing had happened. Everyone went wild with laughter as the grounds crew scrambled to get the car out of the lake. Needless to say, that was the last April Fool's trick played on Larry Parrish.

enough people to have someone throw batting practice. They don't have enough personnel to work with players individually or throw to them under controlled conditions. There aren't enough baseballs, and the money available for other equipment is scarce. As a result, the coaches become very drill-oriented. Most coaches are almost forced to use a lot of drills because they need to break the team into smaller, teachable groups that they can keep busy and working for an entire practice.

A good coach learns how to best work with each hitter, providing the right level of instruction and encouragement.

DRILLS TO DEVELOP A SOLID SWING

The following drills really work and will help young hitters improve. Hitting drills are designed to help a hitter become more efficient at hitting a moving baseball. The hitter's body must learn how to time and recognize all types of pitches. Then the hitter must deliver the bat to the ball and through the ball. All this needs to be accomplished in less than 0.4 second. Now that's an athletic event!

The drills coaches use should work in line with the absolutes of hitting, employ the correct sequence, and deal only with what really happens during a swing. When players use drills that closely simulate reality, they'll be better off.

The number of swings a hitter takes in each practice session and how often a hitter works on his hitting will relate directly to his strength base, age, and desire. It's always better for hitters to take swings in small groups to prevent reaching a fatigue level that may lead to bad habits. Taking turns in small groups allows some recovery time that the hitter needs to maintain his highest bat speed and quickness. Once real fatigue sets in, the hitter will pace himself just to keep swinging. This leads to passive swings that really don't accomplish much. To hit for an hour or until the hands are raw isn't very smart. Quality is better than quantity.

The best drill, if it's at all possible, is to take live batting practice against real pitchers.

Live Batting Practice

Standing in for live batting practice against a real pitcher is the best way to develop pitch recognition and timing. Hitting against a live pitcher is as close to game conditions as a hitter can get.

The hitter needs to stand in against the pitcher as if he were in a game with the whole team counting on him. The hitter should go through his entire batting routine, using the stance he would use in a real game and focusing on the absolutes of hitting and the skills he has learned (figure 10.1).

FIGURE 10.1   Standing in against a pitcher for live batting practice is a good way to develop timing and pitch recognition in a gamelike situation.

The hitter's adrenaline will not be at the level of intensity that it would be in a real game, and he usually will experience a lot of failure. It's extremely important for the hitter to remember the importance of the hitter's attitude. The focus should be on the hitter developing the skill of recognizing good fastballs and breaking balls, and on understanding that this skill will make him better. The hitter shouldn't focus on the immediate results.

Finding live pitching is not easy, as most pitchers have to save themselves to be ready for real games. The next best drill is live batting practice with a coach pitching from a close distance. This drill builds a hitter's confidence while working different areas of the strike zone. This batting practice allows for some control of the situation, and different areas of the strike zone can be worked as needed.

A hitter will experience more success when a coach is pitching to him because the ball will not travel as fast and there will be less movement on the pitch. Usually the hitter feels good when he's done for the day. This is a good hitting-specific drill that also works timing and recognition.

Standing In Against Pitchers During Side Work

This drill, which I mentioned earlier in chapter 5 on recognition, is one of the best ways for a young hitter to learn to recognize pitches and time them.

The hitter stands in the batter's box as the pitcher works all of his pitches but does not swing (figure 10.2). The hitter should always approach the pitch as if he were going to hit it. His back foot comes off first with the bat still over his shoulder. This is the look of a correct take.

This is a tremendous drill that's not used often enough. Hitters have the chance to see fast pitches, breaking balls, and movement over and over again. The quicker the hitter can pick up the ball out of the pitcher's hand (i.e., within the first 5 feet after release) and recognize speed and location, the bigger and slower the ball will look. Remember, a hitter doesn't hit what the pitcher throws; he hits what he sees. The baseball always looks huge to a hitter when he's taking a 3-0 pitch. I believe it could look that way almost all the time. This drill is a must for all hitters high school age and older.

FIGURE 10.2   Standing in during side work.

Swings With an Underloading Bat

The purpose of using an underloading bat—a bat that is 4 to 5 ounces lighter than a regular game bat—is to improve bat speed. In this drill, the hitter attacks live pitches, swinging the bat at high speed. The hitter stands in against a coach tossing softly from behind a safety cage. The hitter works through his entire hitting sequence, concentrating especially on bat speed and quickness. Another option would be for the hitter to use an underloading bat and swing at visualized pitches, focusing on increasing bat speed and quickness with every swing.

By using the underloading bat, the hitter can move his body and hands (in sequence) at a higher-than-normal speed through rotation and the swing. The hitter learns what it feels like for his body and hands to move at a high rate of speed. Over time, the hitter becomes accustomed to that feeling. A small percentage of that speed carries over into the hitter's regular game bat.

Soft Toss

The soft toss drill is commonly used by many players to practice hitting pitches in all areas of the strike zone by altering the bat angle. The coach softly tosses the ball from behind a safety screen set up in front of the hitter. The hitter works through his entire hitting sequence, focusing on changing bat angles to hit pitches in different areas of the strike zone.

This drill teaches the hitter to create energy under controlled conditions. The hitter has the chance to work on bat angles and practice hitting pitches in all areas of the strike zone. The hitter learns contact points and angles for left field, center field, and right field. He also learns how to create bat quickness and speed using the correct hitting sequence.

The soft toss also can be done from the side. The soft toss from the side has much the same purpose as the soft toss drill: to give the hitter experience in hitting pitches in all areas of the strike zone. A coach or a teammate stands to the side of the hitter and tosses the ball softly. The hitter must adjust to each pitch as it comes in at a difficult angle. The person tossing the ball must keep the hitter in a good rhythm but never rush him.

As with the regular soft toss drill, this drill also requires the hitter to hit pitches in all areas of the strike zone. This one is a little more difficult, however, since the hitter must deal with difficult angles because the ball is coming from the side. The person tossing the ball needs to know how to flip it correctly and must keep the hitter in a good rhythm and sequence. The tosser must never rush the hitter. Sometimes players flipping to each other will fire the balls rapidly to get in more swings, but this forces the hitter to use only his upper body, resulting in the development of bad habits.

Hits to an Open Field

Hitting to an open field reinforces good hitting habits and identifies and corrects bad ones. Perform this drill with the tosser standing either behind a screen in front of the hitter or to the side. The tosser softly tosses the ball to the hitter, who hits the ball into the open field. A hitter who tries to hit the ball too hard and uses his upper body too much will hit a lot of ground balls. The hitter needs to relax and use his lower body, feeling his front leg snapping straight just before contact. He needs to finish through the ball and finish high, then watch the ball to see for himself how it carries. Hitters can pair up, two on each side of home plate, and take turns hitting balls to the gaps.

Major league hitters like to use a long tee when they hit into the open field because they can see the results quickly. A hitter learns quickly whether or not he's on time. By using a good hitting sequence and snapping his front leg, the hitter will be able to drive the ball harder and farther. When the hitter tries to muscle up and hits the ball with his upper body, the ball goes nowhere fast.

This drill provides immediate feedback with every swing. The hitter can see exactly how the ball comes off his bat. Hitting errors can be instantly recognized and corrected. When I was coaching in Japan, we used this drill daily. We brought it to the United States, and most hitters really like it.

Tee Work Into a Screen

The purpose of tee work into a screen is to reinforce good hitting mechanics. It is also a good drill to loosen up a hitter. A hitter can use a screen on his own, either while he's awaiting his turn to perform another drill or when he's practicing alone and wants to polish his mechanics.

Using a tee often causes the hitter to keep his head down and his eyes zoned in on the home plate area when the bat makes contact with the ball. The correct way to use a tee is to start by looking out at the pitcher and then track the ball to the tee without a severe backward head movement. The eyes should remain just out in front of the tee and ball.

Dry Swings

Dry swinging is a good way to train a hitter to visualize the pitch. The hitter should use either an underloading bat (one that is 4 or 5 ounces lighter than his game bat) or an overloading bat (one that is 4 ounces heavier than his game bat). Using a lighter bat will train speed; using a heavier bat will train strength. The hitter stands in as if facing a pitcher and swings as if he were really attacking the ball (figure 10.3). With practice, a hitter can visualize breaking balls, splits, and all other types of pitches.

FIGURE 10.3   Dry swings.

This is a great drill when the hitter needs to practice attacking pitches in different areas of the strike zone. Teaching the mind to see all pitches (visualizing) is very important. Doing this drill correctly takes a lot of practice and mental energy. It's not easy for a hitter to visualize pitches and actually see those pitches coming toward him in his mind. The more pitches a hitter can see in his mind and attack correctly, the easier it will be when he sees the real thing in a game.

Aluminum or Wood?

A huge problem for professional scouts is trying to predict if a high school or college player can make the transition from aluminum bats to wood bats. Many good amateur baseball players have been weeded out early in their careers because they couldn't learn how to find the sweet spot on a wooden bat.

Several factors make the transition difficult. First, aluminum bats are usually much lighter than wooden bats, which increases the hitter's bat speed. When the hitter makes contact, a light bat can handle the torque and force. The hitter can hit the pitch harder, and it will travel farther. Second, aluminum bats have a much larger sweet spot than wooden bats. Third, hitters who use aluminum bats rarely experience the feeling of being jammed or breaking the bat. Seldom does a hitter using an aluminum bat feel his hands tingle all the way to first base or have his bat snapped in two by a fastball running in on the hands.

The key to changing from aluminum to wood is to know and feel where the sweet spot is in relation to the hands. It's critical that a batter learn the distance between the hands and the sweet spot, which is constant if the lengths of the bats are the same. This will determine how successful and consistent a hitter he will be in the future.

The sweet spot of a bat is usually about 3 inches below the end of the bat and a few inches above the label, depending on where the label is printed. The entire sweet spot of a wooden bat is about 5 or 6 inches long.

Because aluminum bats have a larger sweet spot, a hitter can get a lot of base hits and line drives that would only be weak pop-ups or broken-bat hits with a wooden bat. The larger sweet spot means the hitter can make contact lower or higher than the real sweet spot and still get a hit. A wooden bat is not as forgiving.

The rules for aluminum bat use have changed over the last few years to make it safer. A strong college or high school player can create such force off an aluminum bat that the pitcher often doesn't have enough time to react to a line drive coming at his face. Adding ounces in relation to the length of the bat could prevent some injuries.

The rule for an aluminum bat is that it must be a minus three. This means that an aluminum bat can weigh only 3 ounces less than its length in inches. For example, a 34-inch aluminum bat must weigh no more than 31 ounces. Older aluminum bats were usually a minus five.

Regardless of the type of bat a hitter uses, he still must learn to be mechanically correct, to be on time, and to recognize all pitches. An aluminum bat can give a hitter a false sense of security. Many serious amateur players today practice with both aluminum and wooden bats, or they find leagues that allow wooden bats. Using wooden bats can result in additional cost because they have a tendency to break if used incorrectly. A player should take advantage of any chance to use a wooden bat. He'll learn more quickly about the relationship between his hands and the sweet spot.

The use of aluminum bats is not always a bad thing, however. Many young hitters, age 7 to 10 years, or hitters who have a weak strength base can benefit from using an aluminum bat. The lighter bat allows a young hitter to feel bat speed and also allows a physically weak hitter to have some success.

As a hitter gets older, he should try to mix in sessions using a wooden bat as often as possible. Experience the joy of a loud, satisfying crack instead of a ping.

DRILLS TO AVOID

Some drills are counterproductive and won't reinforce what really happens during a good swing. In fact, these drills can create bad hitting habits that will be difficult for a hitter to break.

For example, take one-arm drills swinging down through the ball. Swinging down through the ball doesn't happen during a good swing, and this drill teaches the wrong skill. However, when done correctly, the one-arm drill can build strength. Only hitters with a good strength base should try this drill, because a hitter must be strong enough to do it correctly. The one-arm swing has to match the real swing. If swinging with the lead hand—the left hand for a right-handed hitter—the palm must be facing down throughout the entire swing. Rolling the hand over will not teach the correct bat path. If swinging with the top hand—the right hand for a right-handed hitter—the palm must be facing up throughout the entire swing. Rolling the top hand over will not teach the correct bat path.

Many hitters use a very short bat for one-handed swings because it's lighter and easier to get through the hitting zone. The problem with doing so is that the relationship between the hand and the sweet spot of the bat is way out of line. Remember that being aware of the distance between the hands and the sweet spot of the bat is a very important feeling for a hitter.

Also, don't practice off some of the newer tees that have two stems with a ball on each. One ball is higher than the other and must be cleared with the bat for the hitter to hit the lower ball. This teaches a downward or chopping swing, which is a bad habit.

Swinging down doesn't occur during a good swing and shouldn't be taught. When using a tee, always start by looking out to the pitcher and tracking the ball to the tee. Swing through the ball, and let the bat stay in its natural path.

The one-knee drill, in which the hitter takes tomahawk swings at high pitches, also teaches bad habits. A tomahawk or chopping swing at a high pitch, with the bat head above the hands, doesn't happen in a game, so don't practice it. The hands should always be above the ball, and the bat head should always be below the hands at contact. Practice getting the hands over the high pitch and finishing the swing as usual—the hitter should finish high. The bat will always be below the ball on approach, and the hands will always be above the ball at contact.

Avoid taking batting practice against pitching machines at very high speeds. This can really hurt a lot of hitters. A hitter can't develop timing when facing a machine. When the ball speed is high, the hitter doesn't have time to get into full rotation and becomes a top-half-first or hands hitter. If you're using a pitching machine, set it at a slower-than-average speed (around 50 mph) to allow the hitter to make his own timing and be on time so he can practice the correct sequence of the swing. Batting practice against a live pitcher is better.

You don't need to swing a heavy bat during skill work. Swinging a heavy bat is all right for building strength, but when you try to hit a moving baseball from a pitcher or coach, your body will cheat to get to the baseball because it's not strong enough, and poor mechanics will appear. Use a heavy bat for visualization or soft toss only. Be careful when trying to time and attack pitches. A bat that's too heavy will cause the body to commit early just to get the bat head to the ball. Use a heavy bat for strength building only. That means taking dry swings with good balance and using the entire body to deliver the bat.

Rapid-fire soft toss doesn't quicken the hands or the bat speed. It actually slows down bat speed because the hitter cannot get into rotation and will use only his hands and upper body. This is entirely out of sequence and teaches the body incorrectly! When doing soft toss drills, allow the hitter to use his timing as he's getting ready to hit. It may take longer to get in swings, but they'll be on time with correct balance. Allowing the hitter to get on time will help him develop the correct sequence, which by now we know is feet first and hands last.

Conditioning

Today's hitters are proving the positive impact effective conditioning can have on performance at the plate. The power now expected of all position players at the plate reflects the need for any serious athlete in the game to be properly trained if he's going to compete.

Just as good swing mechanics enhance hitting output and consistency, so too can a properly trained physique. To hit with the greatest power and the highest average possible, the body must be conditioned correctly.

Sport-specific training for baseball involves developing the needed energy, muscular strength, aerobic and anaerobic endurance, speed, and agility for optimal performance in the sport. Unfortunately, some players are left in the dugout when it comes to conditioning their bodies for baseball. As a result, many hitters perform at a level below their capabilities.

THE KINETIC ENERGY CHAIN

Similar to sport-specific conditioning, cross-specific training involves matching up the movements performed in a certain athletic task with exercises used to develop strength, power, endurance, and quickness in performing those movements. Functional exercises integrate neuromuscular movements as they occur in executing baseball-specific skills, starting with flexibility exercises, progressing to core training, and finishing with functional cross-specific weight training exercises. This section of the book focuses specifically on functional training for hitting a baseball.

The muscles, nerves, and articular systems of the body function in what is called the *kinetic energy chain*. The kinetic energy chain is the method by which the body transfers kinetic energy through the body into the bat, baseball, or any other object. Essentially, the neuromuscular system is transferring energy through each muscle of your system in a sequential pattern to create an efficient movement.

When a hitter swings a bat, energy created through the stride of his front foot, on contact of that foot with the ground, transfers kinetic

The conditioning information was provided by Sean M. Cochran.

energy sequentially up through the neuromuscular system and out into the bat in an attempt to hit the baseball. Each muscle involved in this sequence absorbs, directs, and delivers energy to the next muscle in line until this energy reaches the bat.

For this energy to be delivered to the bat efficiently with the greatest amount of force, each muscle within the kinetic energy chain must have sufficient neuromuscular strength and endurance to make it happen. If the kinetic energy chain has a weak muscle, then less than an optimal amount of energy will be delivered to the bat, and the weak muscles in the kinetic energy chain will take undue amounts of stress in transferring this energy, potentially resulting in injury.

Think of the body's kinetic energy chain as a chain. If a chain has a weak link in it, and you continually keep pulling on the chain, that one link will eventually break. Your body works in the same fashion. You are only as strong as your weakest link and only as efficient as your poorest mechanic.

Swinging a bat occurs in three dimensions, meaning the body moves in many different directions, and the neuromuscular system is asked to perform in various paths for optimal performance. During the swing, muscles in every part of the body are moving in linear, rotational, and diagonal directions to make the bat move through the contact zone. These muscular actions occur in many different directions, resulting in the coordinated end movement of swinging a bat. For this functional action to occur, we must train the body in all the differing planes of movement in which the action occurs. The three basic planes of movement in which this movement, and any physical action, occurs are the frontal plane (forward-backward), transverse plane (rotation), and sagittal plane (side-side).

The muscles in the body have the ability to perform three different types of actions. All three of these actions are involved concurrently and simultaneously when swinging a bat. Therefore, all three of these movements must be trained for to have consistent, long-term success at the plate.

A concentric muscular action occurs when a muscle in the kinetic chain shortens to transfer energy and accelerate the body. An eccentric muscular action occurs when a muscle in the kinetic chain lengthens to transfer energy and decelerate the body. An isometric contraction occurs when a muscle contracts, creating force without lengthening or shortening. A comprehensive training program requires training all three of these neuromuscular actions.

HITTING-SPECIFIC TRAINING

Now that we know what the body actually does to hit a baseball correctly, we can create a hitting-specific conditioning program. First, let's make sure we're speaking the same language when referring to strength, endurance, and power at the plate.

Neuromuscular strength is the ability of the neuromuscular system to produce force against internal or external resistance. When swinging a bat, the body must remain stable for the hitter to be successful at the plate. If the muscles of the core (low back and abdominals) are weak when striding, the body will be off balance, limiting success at the plate. Conversely, a great deal of neuromuscular core strength will allow the body to remain stable through the stride, resulting in greater success at the plate.

Baseball is a sport of repetition, especially when it comes to hitting. Think of how many times a player swings a bat in a single practice, game, week, or season. A professional player might take 60 to 80 swings in a single day, beginning with tee work and finishing with game at bats. Multiply that out over a week, then a whole season, and you can see the great number of swing repetitions a player can pile up throughout a career.

Every time a player swings a bat, he asks his entire neuromuscular system to repeat the same action over and over again. This becomes quite taxing on the muscular system and requires muscular endurance. If the body is not strong enough or does not have the endurance capacity to maintain the functions required by the sport, then performance will suffer and injury will occur.

Another neuromuscular requirement for hitting is power. Power means creating the greatest amount of force in the least amount of time. Therefore, the two key components of power are strength and speed. A hitter has a fraction of a second to generate maximum force and deliver it into the bat and baseball. Insufficient neuromuscular power distributed into the bat and ball will result in having "warning track power" rather than "home run power."

The final conditioning component crucial to hitting a baseball is balance. When you swing a bat and that front foot lands, kinetic energy is traveling up through your leg, into the torso area, through your shoulder, and into the bat. Large muscles of the legs, small muscles in the torso, and joint-stabilizing muscles of the shoulder are all transferring this energy. The transfer of this energy places stress on all these muscles. Every muscle in this kinetic chain requires the same amount of neuromuscular strength and endurance for the efficient transfer of this energy through the neuromuscular system. If a single muscle is weak, be it a large muscle or joint stabilizer, the result will be less-than-optimal transfer of energy through the kinetic chain and possible injury. If you have muscular imbalances between your large and small muscles, your small muscles will fatigue. The fatigue will result in poor performances at the plate and the eventual breakdown of the muscle.

A comprehensive baseball-specific training program will address neuromuscular balance, strength, endurance, and power training. Table 11.1 indicates the respective training parameters for a hitting-specific conditioning program during the off-season. Adjust the training variables (load, volume, duration, and frequency) to match your desired level of training intensity.

TABLE 11.1   Off-Season Conditioning Program

Type of training	Load and intensity	Exercise speed	Repetitions per set	Duration between sets	Workout frequency
Balance	50 percent or lower	Moderate to fast	6 or more	30 seconds or less	5 or more times per week
Strength	60 to 80 percent	Slow	6 to 12	30 to 60 seconds	4 times per week
Muscular endurance	40 to 70 percent	Moderate	15 or more	60 seconds or less	4 times per week
Endurance	70 percent or lower	Moderate	15 or more	60 seconds or less	2 to 6 times per week
Power	30 to 60 percent	Fast	6 or less	60 to 90 seconds	2 to 4 times per week

Flexibility Training

Flexibility is the range of motion around a joint. Every joint has a range of motion that it should be able to move through to perform the skilled movements of a sport, including hitting a baseball. In training, then, we want to emphasize exercises that are functional in their movements, exercises that are geared toward maintaining the proper range of motion within the joints of the body, and exercises that look to maintain the proper length-tension relationship within the neuromuscular system.

Two types of flexibility training—functional and static stretching—are available to athletes. Functional flexibility exercises prepare the muscles to perform range-of-motion exercises specific to the swing motion a player is going to perform. In other words, functional flexibility can be thought of as a cross-specific warm-up for hitting. Static stretching involves holding a "flexed" position for a period of 10 to 30 seconds. Static stretches are best suited for the cool-down portion of a training program.

Balance and Stabilization Training

Balance is the ability of an individual to maintain control of the body during any given movement. Stabilization is the ability of specific muscles in the neuromuscular system to support or stabilize the body while it performs specific movement patterns.

Being limber is important for hitters, but so is being solid at the base. Balance and stabilization are connected with a certain aspect of conditioning for baseball. They are connected in terms of relevancy and the type of training needed to develop them. Balance cannot be developed without stabilization strength, and stabilization strength cannot be developed without torso training.

The ability to balance and stabilize the body hinges on the development of the torso region. We often see ballplayers perform a great number of abdominal exercises during a workout. This type of training alone does not train the torso region or the body sufficiently for hitting. The torso region of the body includes all the muscles of the pelvis, lumbar area of the spine (low back), and abdominal region. The abdominal structure is only one part of the torso region, and as discussed earlier, the entire body (i.e., kinetic chain) must be trained to create balance throughout the neuromuscular system.

Torque

Torque is defined as the amount of force through the rotation of a joint. The pertinence of the torque principle in terms of baseball becomes quite evident when looking at a swing. A great amount of torque is developed in the torso region when swinging a bat. As a result, the torso region must be trained for torque development in a baseball-specific training program.

If one muscle (large muscle, small muscle, synergist, stabilizer) is weak, it will break down as a result of the stresses placed on it during activity. Performance will suffer, and injury will eventually occur. Joint integrity training focuses on developing the neuromuscular capacities of the synergist and stabilizer muscles that surround the joints of the body. Quite often the "weak link" in the neuromuscular system occurs in the joint capsule areas of the body. Ask yourself one question: Where do the majority of injuries occur in baseball? The answer is: in the joint capsules of the kinetic chain. A joint integrity segment must be incorporated within your baseball-specific training program.

FUNCTIONAL BASEBALL TRAINING PROGRAM GUIDELINES

We have discussed the importance of the kinetic chain, functional exercises, and cross-specific training. This is the point in the training program where these principles are essential. We know that baseball is a "feet to fingertip" sport, and that every muscle in the kinetic chain is being utilized either concentrically, eccentrically, or isometrically to create the given athletic movement. We understand that for optimal performance between the lines, training modalities must mirror the neuromuscular actions during competition (i.e., cross-specific training). We have created the foundation of a training program with modalities that agree with these principles, but now what do we do to incorporate exercises that train the larger muscles (the prime movers) of the neuromuscular system?

Remember that the manner of training must be cross-specific to the movement patterns associated with baseball. We need to train the kinetic chain of the body with multiplanar, multidirectional, isometric, concentric, and eccentric exercises. The exercises should focus on developing the neuromuscular capacities of endurance, strength, and power specific to the sport of baseball, training the body as a unit, not in isolated parts. We all know that baseball is a sport in which the entire neuromuscular system is used to hit, throw, field, and run. Therefore, the body must be trained as a single unit.

The following information describes a set of principles we want to use in determining the specific exercises and protocols to be incorporated into a baseball-specific training program. Baseball hitting requires that all of these physical capacities be addressed: power, endurance, strength, strength endurance, balance, and stabilization. Multidimensional training (table 11.2) must be incorporated into the training program to address all of these areas.

Baseball hitting is a multidirectional skill in which the body moves through multiple planes (sagittal, frontal, transverse) to perform the athletic actions of the game. A training program must incorporate multiplanar exercises to be cross-specific to the requirements of the game (table 11.3).

TABLE 11.2   Multidimensional Training for Hitting

Type of training	Sample exercise	Sets and repetitions	Exercise speed
Power	Medicine ball side throw	1 to 2 sets of 15 repetitions	Fast
Endurance	Light dumbbell exercises	1 set of 15 or more repetitions	Slow
Strength	Physio-ball dumbbell press	1 to 2 sets of 8 repetitions	Moderate
Strength endurance	Standing lat pulldown	1 to 2 sets of 12 repetitions	Slow
Balance	Single-leg cone touch	1 set of 15 repetitions	Moderate
Stabilization	Physio-ball crunches	1 set of 15 or more repetitions	Moderate

TABLE 11.3 Multiplanar Movement Training for Hitting

Exercise	Movement plane	Sets and repetitions	Movement speed
Rotational lunges	Transverse and sagittal	1 to 2 sets of 8 to 12 repetitions	Moderate
Medicine ball diagonal chops	Frontal, sagittal, and transverse	1 to 2 sets of 15 repetitions	Fast
Rotational dumbbell press	Sagittal and transverse	1 to 2 sets of 8 to 12 repetitions	Moderate
Side-to-side cone hops	Frontal	1 to 2 sets of 15 or more repetitions	Fast

A training program for baseball requires the exercises and protocols within the program to mimic the athletic actions of the sport. This allows for what is termed a *transfer of training effect* to occur. A cross-specific training program (table 11.4) allows for the neuromuscular improvements made during a training program to be transferred to improved performance during competition.

A training program must continually challenge the athlete's levels of neuromuscular endurance, strength, strength endurance, power, balance, and core stabilization for advancement to be made. If planned increases in the difficulty of the program and exercises are not integrated into the functional training program, improvement by the athlete will be inhibited. Table 11.5 shows a good exercise progression for a hitter in training.

A functional program follows a series of steps in which the athlete begins with developing the parameters of flexibility within the neuromuscular system, proceeds to the development of balance and stabilization capacities, progresses to the development of joint integrity and core strength, and completes the program with functional weight training modalities. Table 11.6 shows a systematic progression of a hitter's total training plan.

Eccentric, concentric, and isometric contractions all must be trained in a functional hitting program. Doing so will allow for the greatest force output within the neuromuscular system (table 11.7).

TABLE 11.4   Cross-Specific Training for Hitting

Exercise	Cross-specific activity	Sets and repetitions	Movement speed
Dumbbell lunge with a reach	Fielding ground ball in the hole	1 to 2 sets of 8 to 12 repetitions	Moderate
Medicine ball side throw	Rotation of torso as in hitting	1 to 2 sets of 15 repetitions	Fast
Dumbbell step-ups	Lower body action in sprinting	1 to 2 sets of 8 to 12 repetitions	Moderate to fast

TABLE 11.5   Exercise Progression for Hitter's Training

Sample exercise	Progression #1	Progression #2	Progression #3
Physio-ball dumbbell press	Two-arm simultaneous press	Two-arm alternating press	One-arm press
Dumbbell squat	Two-leg squat	One-leg squat	Two legs unstable surface* squat
Lat pulldown	Seated two-arm pulldown	Staggered standing position two-arm pulldown	One-leg standing position two-arm pulldown
Dumbbell deadlift	Two-leg deadlift	One-leg deadlift	Two legs unstable surface* deadlift

* An unstable surface, such as a Dyna Disc, should be used.

TABLE 11.6 Systematic Progression of Total Training for Hitting

Program number	Balance exercise	Stabilization exercise	Core exercise	Joint integrity exercise	Functional exercise
1	Single-leg cone touch	Prone position holds	Physio-ball Russian twist	Elastic tubing exercises	Multi-directional lunges
2	Single-leg squat	Staggered position push-up	Seated medicine ball twist	Light dumbbell exercises	Physio-ball single-arm dumbbell press
3	Single-leg deadlift	Physio-ball table top	Medicine ball chops	Medicine ball wall throws	Single-leg lat pulldowns

TABLE 11.7 Force Output Spectrum

Category	Sample exercise	Sets and repetitions	Movement speed
Isometric	Prone position holds	1 set of 30 to 60 seconds	No movement
Concentric	Physio-ball two-arm alternating dumbbell press	1 to 2 sets of 8 to 12 repetitions	Moderate
Eccentric	Medicine ball side throw	1 to 2 sets of 15 repetitions	Fast

IN-SEASON AND OFF-SEASON HITTER TRAINING

We've covered principles and provided sample exercises for a hitting-specific training program. But all that information doesn't mean a thing if the athlete fails to use it. Success as a hitter in today's game requires year-round training. Training hard in the off-season and performing only on-the-field baseball activities (no weight training) during the season will result in a gradual decrease in performance as the season progresses and a higher risk of injury. In-season and off-season baseball training programs do differ, but both are essential for optimal performance.

The greatest difference between in-season and off-season programs is the volume or amount of work performed. Volumes are generally lower during the season and higher in the off-season. During the season, it is best to perform a small volume daily. The off-season allows us to create a much larger volume of work. Use the guidelines in table 11.8

TABLE 11.8 In-Season and Off-Season Training Guidelines

Type of training	In-season program	Off-season program
Flexibility	7 times per week	7 times per week
Balance	6 times per week	6 times per week
Stabilization	2 times per week	6 times per week
Joint integrity	6 times per week	6 times per week
Functional endurance	2 times per week	2 to 6 times per week
Functional strength	2 times per week	2 to 6 times per week
Functional power	1 to 2 times per week	2 to 4 times per week

for developing effective in-season and off-season training programs that will benefit you at the plate and in other areas of your baseball performance.

FINAL THOUGHTS

We've gone over a lot of information in this book, from a hitter's attitude all the way to making contact with the pitch, from breaking down the swing to practice and conditioning. The important factors involved in hitting a baseball, such as timing, recognition, and attacking, have been discussed again and again. You've heard over and over how the legs and correct movement sequence are so important to a hitter and how energy is translated from the feet up to the hands and finally out to the bat head.

Now, what are you as a hitter or coach going to do with this information?

A hitter has to have motivation to move up to the next level and take the next step to better competition. A coach has to be motivated to take his players to the next level and give them the information and confidence that will stay with them forever.

Watching and understanding videotape is one of the best available teaching tools in baseball today for coaches and hitters alike. The use of video is essential if we are going to give hitters the best opportunity to develop their talents. It also gives coaches and hitters a chance to see what really happens when it comes to hitting a baseball. We are coaching in the dark ages if we feel we can do without video.

Good players take the time and effort to keep themselves strong and fit during the off-season or school breaks. Physical conditioning is very important for any athlete, especially baseball players. Playing baseball in itself doesn't keep a player physically fit. A player must do extra work, and smart work, to excel. Hitters must spend time working the body to prepare it for good, aggressive swings at high speed.

At some point, a player will also have to deal with an injury that interferes with his playing time for a while. The level of conditioning you've reached before an injury can determine how fast you'll bounce back. Always get good advice when injured, and don't try to work through pain. If any part of your body doesn't loosen up after a good warm-up session, you should get that part checked out. Work hard and be smart about conditioning!

Everything you do will be tempered by your attitude. Take the best information in the world, use it, and be as good as your potential will allow. As a hitter, you may hear people say you can't hit feet first, hands last. They'll tell you that the hands are the most important part of hitting. You may hear little about rotation and sequence. It's up to you to decide what's important and what's not. You have the ammunition now to make the right decisions. Always listen to your coach, as he'll make suggestions that can help you succeed. Just be smart and filter out any information that you know won't help.

Saying Goodbye

I was coaching with the Texas Rangers in 1992. The season was winding down, and we were in Anaheim for our last game of the year. Brian Downing was retiring after that game.

After Brian got a hit on his first or second at-bat, he was pulled from the game to a standing ovation by the Anaheim fans. Brian had had a great career in Anaheim, and the fans remembered his fierce competitiveness and talent.

Brian was a special player and a real character. He loved his Harley Davidson motorcyles and sometimes traveled with the Hell's Angels during the winter months. He rode his Harley to the park in Texas quite a bit and usually wore a leather vest with no shirt. Brian lived only a few miles from the stadium in Anaheim, so on the day of his last game he rode his Harley to the stadium. When the game was over, everyone said goodbye, and the rest of the team boarded the buses that would take us to LAX for the return flight to Arlington.

I was riding in the second bus when I heard a loud rumbling sound alongside the bus. There was Brian on one of his high-rise Harley Davidson motorcycles, holding a Texas Rangers baseball hat in one hand as he pulled alongside the bus. He raised his cap to all of us, popped the gas, and shot up to the first bus and did the same thing. Everyone was shouting and screaming at him through the windows. We all had chills as he rode by and, with precise timing, veered off into the sunset for the last time at the exit leading to his house. It was a great ending to a great career. I haven't seen him since, but I still get chills when I replay that sight in my mind.

With the information we've covered, a lot of hard work, and a lot of fun, any player can become a better hitter and have a chance to achieve the goals he has set for himself. Take this information and go for it! Remember, playing baseball is fun. Don't let a fear of failure keep you from working your hardest to be the best you can be. Never be afraid to swing and miss. Never doubt for a second that you can hit!

INDEX

Note: An italicized *t* following a page number refers to a table.

A

Adair, Robert 26
aggressive hitting. *See* power hitting
agility. *See* flexibility
Alou, Moises 30
aluminum bats 144-145
anticipation, in recognition skills 64-65, 68
arm movement/location
    effects on rotation 72, 78-79
    in high finish 108-112, 116
arm slot, pitcher's, in recognition skills 61-62
arrogance, confidence *vs.* 4, 9
art, of hitting xv, 26, 64, 78
articular system, kinetic energy chain of 150-151, 153, 156
attacking
    axis of rotation impact on 71-73, 78
    balance for 51-54
    definition of 70-71
    with high finish 108-109
    the high pitch 89-90
attitude 1-13
    for busting out of a slump 9-11
    confidence as 4-9
    of experienced hitters 1-4
    measurement of 5
    physical conditioning and 161-162
    real definition of 4-9
    for returning from injury 11-13
    of young hitters 7, 9
axis of rotation, vertical
    belly button in 71-72
    center of gravity in 72-73, 76
    definition of 71
    energy translation and 78-79, 84
    impact on attacking 71-73, 78
    necessity of 46, 71, 96
    during swing timing 31, 37

B

backward pitches 68
bad-ball hitters 17

bad calls 22
bad habits, preventing 11
Bagwell, Jeff 30
balance 45-54
    breaking ball and 53-54
    dynamic. *See* dynamic balance
    hitting-specific training for 154
        neuromuscular 152-153
        off- *vs.* in-season programs 153, 153*t*, 160*t*
    learning by feeling 16
    rebuilding after injury 11
    striding to. *See* stride to balance
    during swing timing 27, 31, 36-39
    value of 2, 10, 46, 51, 96
bat(s)
    aluminum *vs.* wood 144-145
    holding. *See* grip
    individual preferences for 121-122, 144-146
    sweet part of 56, 96-97, 146
    underloading, for practice 141
bat angles
    for bunting 126-127, 130
    correct 68
    in high finish 109, 118
    for high pitch 99-100
    for inside pitch 97-98
    for low pitch 100
    for outside pitch 97
    in situational strategy 96-97, 118
    strike zone and 97-99, 141
bat handle, how to hold. *See* grip
bat head, in angling strategy 96-99
bat lag
    definition of 10, 79, 101-102
    in high finish 109
    necessity of 46, 96
    technique for contact 96, 102-104
bat length, individual preferences for 121-122
bat quickness, bat speed *vs.* 89
bat speed

commitment to 2, 162-163

cross-specific training for 150, 156-157, 158t

definition of 2

functional training for 150-151, 155-157, 156t-159t

hitting-specific training for 152-155, 153t

of Japanese hitters 73-74

value of xiii, xvi, 150, 152, 161

confidence

as good hitter's attitude 4-9

methods for gaining 5, 67

contact

in bat lag technique 96, 102-103

in high finish 108-112, 116-117, 119

control, mental, as experienced focusing 10, 16-17, 19, 22-23

coordination, as balance component 46

cross-specific training 150, 156-157, 158t

crouching, at plate 50, 87

D

desire, as competitor quality 5, 7

determination, of young players 7, 9

dipping 91, 134

discipline, commitment to 2, 162-163

distortion, in recognition skills 60

doubt. *See* negative thoughts

Downing, Brian 2, 162

drag bunt 127

drills, for practice 135

to avoid 145-147

to develop solid swing 137-145

miscellaneous examples of 19, 22, 37, 131

dry swings, in batting practice 143-144

dynamic balance

definition of 46, 48

in full swing for high finish 113

necessity of 10, 46, 51, 96

with power hitting 77-78, 84

timing and 27, 31, 36

E

eccentric muscle contraction 151, 155

functional training for 157, 159t

education, of young players xiv-xv, 7, 16, 31

elbow position

in high finish 109-110

individual preference for 123

elite players. *See* experienced hitters

endurance

hitting-specific training for 150, 152-155

off- *vs.* in-season programs 153, 153t, 160t

kinetic energy chain in 150-151

energy

balance component of 46

displacement with foot landing 36-37

dynamic balance for 46, 51, 84

rotation for 76-78, 84-85

displacement with hitting 152-153

hitting-specific training for 150

kinetic chain of 150-151, 153, 156

rotation component of 71-72, 76-81

front-side blocking in 84-85

exercise progression, for hitting training 157, 158t

experienced hitters

attacking by 70

attitude of 1-4

good elements of 4-9, 120, 134, 161

mental focus skills of 10, 16-17, 19, 22-23

personal preference and style of 120-123

recognition skills of 56-58

extension

in high finish 109-111

in stride timing 35

eyes and eye contact

with bat angling 100

for bunting 126, 128

in recognition skills 57-58, 60-64, 67

in rotation skills 72-73, 84, 86

F

failure, learning how to handle 9-11, 134, 139

fastballs

front-side blocking for hitting 86-87

getting jammed by 75

recognition of 56, 64, 68, 139

turning on 86

fatigue 139, 152-153

fear, learning how to overcome 26, 115, 129

feeling, as learning mechanism 16

feeling sorry for yourself 11

feet movement/position

torso, in rotation 71-72, 79-81
toughness
    mental. *See* mental skills
    physical. *See* conditioning
tracking, as tool for focusing 20, 60
traditional stride, with kick and tap, as
        timing trigger 31-39
training
    sport-specific. *See* hitting-specific
        training
    of young players xiv-xv, 7, 16
transfer of training effect 157
trash talk, confidence *vs.* 4-5, 9
"turn it on" 86
two-strike hitting, recognition skills for
        66-67

U
underloading bat, for practice 141
upper body
    in front-side blocking 84-86, 91
    in rotation skills 79-80
uppercut 134

V
Valentine, Bobby xiv, 26, 135
velocity, of swing. *See* bat speed
Ventura, Robin 12-13

videotaping, as teaching tool 91-93,
        161
visualization
    for focusing 19-20, 23
    for recognition skills 64

W
warm-up sessions, focus during 22
weight. *See* body weight
weight training. *See* strength building
wide-eyed vision, recognition skills and
        63
Williams, Ted xiii, 60
wood bats 144-145
work ethic, as competitor quality 5

Y
young hitters
    attacking by 70-71
    attitude of 7, 9
    education of xiv-xv, 7, 16
    kick development in 31
    mental focus skills of 16-17
    motivation of xiv-xv, 7, 9
    personal preference and style of
        120-123
    swing checklist for 91-93

ABOUT THE AUTHOR

As a Major League hitting coach for 12 years, Tom Robson knows what it takes to become a great hitter. A former Minor League Player of the Year and Pacific Coast MVP, Robson has coached hundreds of big leaguers, including Rafael Palmeiro, John Olerud, and Mike Piazza.

Robson works with Bio-Kinetics, a company that uses computer-generated, three-dimensional motion analysis to help athletes maximize performance through proper biomechanics. He lives in Tempe, Arizona.

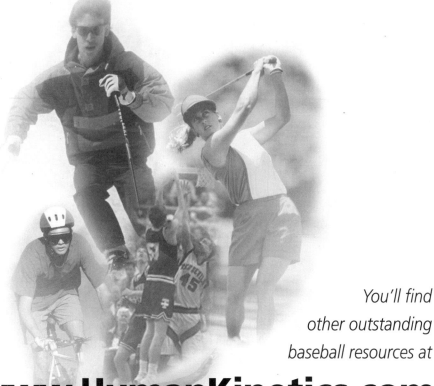